THE POETRY TRIALS

HERTFORDSHIRE & ESSEX

Edited by Lisa Adlam

First published in Great Britain in 2016 by:

Remus House
Coltsfoot Drive
Peterborough
PE2 9BF
Telephone: 01733 890066
Website: www.youngwriters.co.uk

All Rights Reserved
Book Design by Ashley Janson
© Copyright Contributors 2015
SB ISBN 978-1-78624-061-3
Printed and bound in the UK by BookPrintingUK
Website: www.bookprintinguk.com

FOREWORD

Welcome, Reader!

For Young Writers' latest competition, *The Poetry Trials*, we gave secondary school students nationwide the challenge of writing a poem. They were given the option of choosing a restrictive poetic technique, or to choose any poetic style of their choice. They rose to the challenge magnificently, with young writers up and down the country displaying their poetic flair.

We chose poems for publication based on style, expression, imagination and technical skill. The result is this entertaining collection full of diverse and imaginative poetry, which is also a delightful keepsake to look back on in years to come.

Here at Young Writers our aim is to encourage creativity in the next generation and to inspire a love of the written word, so it's great to get such an amazing response, with some absolutely fantastic poems. It made choosing the winners extremely difficult, so well done to *Miracle Okereke* who has been chosen as the best in this book. Their poem will go into a shortlist from which the top 5 poets will be selected to compete for the ultimate Poetry Trials prize.

I'd like to congratulate all the young poets in *The Poetry Trials – Hertfordshire & Essex* – I hope this inspires them to continue with their creative writing.

Jenni Bannister

Editorial Manager

CONTENTS

Vithusha Sivaneswaran (17) 1
Zainab Bedar (13) 2
Sabah Athar (14) 3
Aleksandra Wozniak (12) 4

Dame Alice Owen's School, Potters Bar
Aditya Sembian (12) 5
Ciara Griffin (12) 6
Harry James Dewberry (13) 7
Elly Sturmy (12) 7

Greensward Academy, Hockley
Minnie Harris (11) 8
Charlotte Wallace (11) 9
Alarna Baker (11) 10
Evie Hilliard-Fisher (12) 11
Claudia Pergande (11) 12
Oliver Nicks (12) 12
Laura Smiles 13
Matteo Aylott (11) 13
Bethany Carlow (11) 14
Kayleigh Barrett (11) 14
Beth Rawlings (11) 15
Noah Denton (11) 15
Hannah Bibby (11) 16
Logan Miller (11) 16
Beatrix Pattenden (11) 17
Nathan Player (11) 17
Maddie Collins (11) 18
Katie Slaughter (11) 18
Flinn Cattanach Ashdown (12) 19
Elizabeth Potter (12) 19
Genevieve Booth (11) 20
Jacob Wardle (11) 20
Sam Fenwick 21

Hertswood Academy, Borehamwood
Raffaele Marra (12) 22
Habibah Islam (12) 23
Joanna Armistead (14) 24
Jessica Bruce 25

Daisy Elicia Ferozha-Warwick (12) 25
Kira Reed (12) 26
Morgan-Paige Basham 26
David Delia (12) 27
Savannah Endean (12) 27
Becky Leech (12) 28
Matilda Shkupi 28
Kerri-Anne Morris (12) 29
Ellen Tester (14) 29
Alfie Basham (12) 30
Lucas Gannon (12) 30
Belle Shannon 31
Tajbir Singh 31
Holly Graber (14) 32
Christina Angus 32
Lauren Holmes 33
Paige Shadbolt (12) 33
Bleon Shalaku 34
Hayley-Jade John (12) 34
Levi Kane (14) 35

Immanuel College School, Bushey
Sabrina Miller (15) 35

Kings Langley School, Kings Langley
Lucy Packman (13) 36
Rosanna Rushton (12) 37
Robyn Stevenson (13) 38
Beth Edwards (12) 39
Bethany Howard (13) 40
Megan Goodall (13) 41
Holly Bradshaw (12) 42
Jack Hancock (13) 43
Danny McCarthy (13) 43

Marriotts School, Stevenage
Shenelle Davis 44
Harry Welham (13) 45
Tess Xiao (12) 46
Maddison Malocco (11) 47
Carmel Corpe (11) 47

Ellie Price (12) 48
Rosie-Mae Blackie (11) 48
Courtney Daly (11) 49

Passmores Academy, Harlow

Michael Archer (14) 49
Georgia Moore (14) 50
Mollie Johns (14) 51
Daria Stoszek (14) 52
Becky Melanie Shaw (14) 53
Gracey Dorling (14) 54
Claudia Agnes (14) 55
James Wright (15) 56
Rianna Samuels (14) 57
Kyra Jayne Hiett (14) 58
Shana Barrows (14) 59
Kieran Berry (14) 60
Megan Slater (14) 60
Nicole Delanbanque (14) 61
Samuel Cleverdon (14) 61
Emily Hills (15) 62
Skye Perkins (14) 62
Charlotte May Chiraghuddin (14) 63
Brittany Russell (14) 63
Jake Balding (14) 64
Emma Oakes (14) 64
Jade Smith (14) 65
Jed Harrison (14) 65
Isabella Curtis (14) 66
Robyn Groom (14) 66
Jack Grey (14) 67
Emma Keoghoe
& Alice Olivia Larraine Brock (14) 67
Ellie Morgan (15) 68
Jasmine Burt (14) 68
Emily Evans (14) 69
Bradley Hayden Arnold (14) 69
Robyn Iona Fell (14) 70
Kimberley Airlie (14) 70
George Bright (14) & Lewis 71
Robert Judd (15) 71
Hallie Green (14)
& Marilia Sofia Pais De Abreu
Costa (15) 72
Kayleigh Woods (14) 72
Shannon Pickering (14) 73
Bailey Spencer Nicklen (14) 73

Rebecca Porter (14) 74
Macy Hannaford (14) 74
Hollie Dawson (14) 75
Kaylee Samuels (15) 75
Susie Green (14) 75
Tom Brown (14) 76
Rebecca Richardson (15) 76
Drew Cooper (14) 76
Jaz Harvey (14) 77
Sam Marston 78
Owen Sharpe (14) 78

St Albans Girls' School, St Albans

Harriet Wakefield (11) 79
Mashiath Choudhury (15) 80
Emma Durkin (11) 81
Louise Deans (11) 82
Emily Frangiskou-Hemming (14) 84
Irsa Khan (14) 85
Rachel Staples (11) 86
Chloe May Southall (11) 87
Samiha Thakur (12) 88
Ranya Ramdani (11) 88
Marika Stefani (11) 89
Elena Cobb (11) 89
Emily Branston (11) 90
Kayleigh Hardwick (11) 90
Mahjabeen Choudhury (11) 91
Amelie Wood (12) 91
Amber Durrant (11) 92
Abby Farnsworth (11) 92
Shakhreen Thoyeba Miah (11) 93
Sophia Laycock (13) 93
Kirsty Reed (12) 94
Jemima Biodun-Bello (13) 94
Millie Walker (11) 95

St Benedict's Catholic College, Colchester

Danielle Martin 96
Bandi Cserep (12) 97
Maddie Barrell (11) 98
Amaia Lilia Jane D'Souza (12) 98
Zylo Green 99
Inge-Maria Christine Botha (12) 99
Shannon Payne 100

Tom Brown 100
Natasha Gail Escabarte 101
Chenile Sulley 101
Olivia Farry 102

Tabor Academy, Braintree

Kyeron David Holmes (11) 102
Freddy Braniff (11) 103
Katie Lesiak 104
Brooke Moore 105
Ellie Stewart (11) 105
Alisha Oddy 106
Freddie Wacey 106
Charlie Archer (11) 107
William Henry Pegrum (13) 107
Jack Pinner 108
Rachel Huxter 108
Demi Castell 109
Joseph Little 109
Mae Warner (12) 110
Freddy Thorogood 110
Elisha Elliston 111
Daniella Noble 111
Jessica Rose Stewart (11) 112
Dexter Love 112
Isabelle Louis (11) 113
Josh Stone 113
Isobel Watson 114
Nathan Innes (11) 114
Daisy Eastman (11) 115

The Chauncy School, Ware

Lana Josephine Donovan (12) 115
Kavinaya Shree Sivakumar (12) 116
Amy Gent (11) 117
Josh Thomas Davies (13) 118
Thomas Protherough (11) 119
Roseanna Drake (12) 120
John Drake (11) 121
Alana Romagnoli (15) 122
Olivia Cotgrave (12) 123
Evie Gaze (11) 124
Thomas Offord (13) 125
Katie Davies (12) 126
Rebekka Carter Elliott (12) 127
Keelan Peake (11) 128

Isabel Ogunyemi (12) 128
Emily Grace Weatherall (15) 129

Valentines High School, Ilford

Simranjit Sekhon (11) 129
Arunan Nadarajah (11) 130
Zarmina Usman Khanzada (11) 131
Harris Bidiwala (12) 132
Muhtasim Abrar 133
Rameez Taha Haider (11) 134
Aysha Hussain (11) 135
Ishrak Sarar Hossain 136
Denesh Kannalingam (11) 137
Mahnoor Malik (11) 138
Arda Kuskaya 139
Zaid Shanawaz (12) 140
Ria A Gola (11) 140
Hussain Seedat (11) 141
Harjeevan Panesar (11) 141
Tanisa Karim (11) 142
Dev Vora (12) 142
Sophie Midlane (12) 143
Sasha Sood (11) 143
Jaha Falak Khan 144
Mohammad Sheriff (12) 144
Arjun Jandu (12) 145
Hemang Warudkar (11) 145
Nikita Abedin (11) 146
Rabeena Raveendrakumar 146
Urbi Haidar (12) 147
Imran Ibrahim (11) 147
Neil Patel (11) 148
Khadiza Rahman (11) 148
Abida Yasminn (11) 149
Kamal Shoble 149
Lina Khemili (12) 150
Yash Dhamija (12) 150
Danis Maninathan 151
Amina Mumtaz Qaisar (12) 151
Sydney Massey (11) 152
Renyl Rathan Selwyn (11) 152
Veda Jayne Harrison (12) 153
Warda Naman (13) 153
Nakhal Furqan (11) 154
Yusuf Khankhara (11) 154
Jeni Tanushi (11) 155

Amelia Hynds (12)	155
Zaiba Adam (12)	156
Jeremy Sanchez-Londono (12)	157
Elise Hassan Islam (12)	158
Kirit Sehmbi	158
Elisha Nansri Bailey (11)	159
Ibraheem Ansari (12)	159
Tringa Baca	160
Zainah Hussain (11)	161
Hassan Mahmood (11)	162
Shaheera Uddin (11)	163
Mohammed Zaid Kidia (11)	164
Umar Salam (11)	164
Maheen Khalid (12)	165
Luqmaan Khan (11)	165

Westfield Academy, Watford

Amy Harland (14)	166

THE POEMS

DON'T LEAVE ME HERE ALONE

Running through the dark, cold streets of London,
Laughter of the two boys, leaning against the wall, echoed.
Now I stand here, all alone,
With the harsh wind slicing across my skin.
Now I know that these are the few memories I have left of you, of us.
Because you are gone, you are not in this world anymore.

My world was dark, hidden beneath a shadow,
I reflected it, by being cruel and dark, so I let no one close.
Thus I spat bitter words, with my cold gaze on you,
You kept your gentle smile and amused glance like it was nothing.
You held out your hand, an offer of friendship,
I took hold of it, clinging to the only warmth that I had.

You, my friend, were the opposite of me,
You had the purest heart, a gift to treasure.
In your eyes alone, you found goodness in me,
Past the deep, dark, depth of my soul.
You were the light, in my shadow world,
You were the friend, who just understood and didn't judge.

You pulled me out of the deep waters, which crashed against me.
With you as my support, it was easier to look above it, to face against it.
But death was even crueller than me, he took you away,
And without your support, once again I plunged into darkness, drowning.
How can one stay above the water without help?
How can one live in the world, without half of its soul?

Slowly I emerged from the water,
Because I knew, despite everything, whatever I did, you were there.
I still hear your melodic chuckle and hear your soft warning,
No matter what, you are still that steady flame by my side, consistent and sincere.
Even with the gaping hole in my heart, one that will never fill,
Just know that you were my friend, you were my brother.

Vithusha Sivaneswaran (17)

HERO

'All writers are sad.'
I believe all sad people write,
My first wish, my first wish is the most important,
My first wish is happiness,
And don't even dare give me a pity glance,
Or even offer me a mask,
I ask for one thing and I ask for happiness.
Don't try to give me anything else.

'You'll learn to love yourself.'
It's not easy,
It's not easy I say as I tell you my second wish,
My second wish is to self-respect,
Lately I've been looking in the mirror unable to recognise myself,
I've been looking in the mirror to see a world of tornados,
I've been looking in the mirror to see someone I hate,
I wish to look in the mirror and be proud, and have respect for myself.

'Just one wish is enough'
Nothing is ever 'enough',
We learn how to accept the 'satisfactory',
My third wish you will laugh at,
My third wish is an infinite amount of wishes,
My third wish, it means so much,
Whether it be wishing for my family to be financially well,
Whether it be wishing for my best friend to finally meet her favourite band,
I need an infinite amount of wishes.

'Your parents will be proud of you no matter what.'
It's not like that
I understand what you're saying
But there's so much more than making your parents somewhat proud,
My fourth wish is to have my parents proud of me,
I want them to hold pride for me in their hearts,
I want to be able to provide for my parents,
I just want them to be genuinely proud of me.

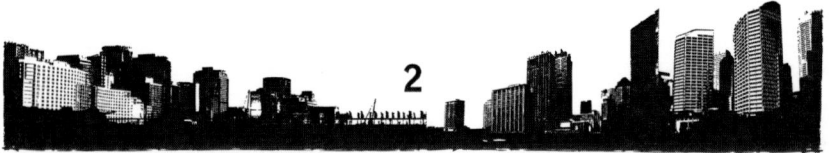

'You are not scared of the action but the consequence.'
I agree.
I'm not scared of love, just heartbreak,
My last wish is never ending love,
There is no need for an explanation.

Zainab Bedar (13)

BAD, BAD DAY

The alarm didn't ring,
The shower didn't do its thing
The soap slipped away,
And I ran out of hair spray
My clothes wouldn't straighten out,
The bedroom door ignored my shout
And trapped my finger,
So I had to linger
There by the door,
Listening to my brother snore.
The toaster was jammed,
The front door slammed,
And my hot coffee spilled onto my hand.

My car's being stubborn,
My boss' got heartburn
So there's no one to govern,
And I've lost my intern.
None of the work is finished,
The staple supply's diminished,
The printer won't print,
Someone's blocked the sink,
The toilets stink,
I'm on the brink!

My umbrella flies away,
The rain destroys my aunt's souffle,
The house is in disarray,
What a bad, bad day!

Sabah Athar (14)

DEADLINE

Darkness around me... though light I see
Silence so loud I can't hear myself think
The trials are ending right now, right here
Suddenly footsteps are what I hear...

They're coming! They're here, I must conceal
Run away from their sight
But instead I run and don't look back...

I run with my heart pumping
Banging on my chest,
Through the maze of not knowing where

I pass ivy's witch fingers
Trees' wrinkly feet
I run and run not daring to stop
Not daring to look back at the disease
I run and run hearing blood in my ears.

Hearing it coming near
I run in terror of meeting it
Face to face seeing it

I run until I stop in fear
It's the end of my journey now
Soon I will only be a lifeless crop
Laying on the bloody floor

That's it, not long now only a minute or two
And it will catch me staring into its eyes
I have reached my final stage; I will be free soon...

I can see it now getting near...
I would dream of running off
Into the world's safe hands
Into my home
But it is simply impossible as I have reached the end
My deadline is here...

Aleksandra Wozniak (12)

AT THE ZOO

At the zoo, there are many animals,
Lions, tigers, gorillas and camels,
A zoo can be very loud,
Just like the uproar of a crowd

Lions may look very cute,
But in truth, they can be brutes.
They have the fangs of a snake,
They can easily cut through raw steak.

Elephants are huge creatures,
That have unusual features,
They are navy grey,
And ten times tougher than potter's clay.

Monkeys can be cheeky,
But they are definitely not freaky,
They are charming beasts,
Who love to have feasts.

Zebras are striped,
And very highly liked,
A zebra's stripes are black and white,
And sometimes, they are known to bite!

The zoo is a wonderful place to visit,
Where there are insects like crickets
This is to name but a few,
Of the wonderful animals populating the zoo!

Aditya Sembian (12)
Dame Alice Owen's School, Potters Bar

NO ONE

Wails, all around, no room left to move.
The flies buzz around the corpses,
And the nurses hold their breath.
And in her silence, no one sees her.

No one will go to help them,
No one will go to a charity,
But everyone will sigh
And thank the heavens it's not them.

Her eyes are unseeing,
Yet as she dies, her soul sits up.
She wanders, and he watches, uncertain.
He ponders how no one can notice her death.

No one will know the little orphan girl's joy,
No one will know her name,
But the little boy will know,
Her soul was taken by an angel.

And many years later,
His young and joyful soul,
Will leave his old and weary body,
And everyone will mourn him.

No one will see the soft smile on his face,
No one will see the spirit that he sees,
But the old man sees
The girl who died and became an angel.

Ciara Griffin (12)
Dame Alice Owen's School, Potters Bar

READING ADVENTURE

If thou requires help,
There lacks a place better to reach,
Than in a reading adventure.

Many brimmed with terrific tales,
Travelling beautiful, magical lands,
Full with greatness and villains and happily ever afters.

Many written with facts plenty,
Facts vaster than the stars in the sky,
While thou reads and takes in anew.

When thou has a rest,
Just reel thy decisions,
Relax and immerse thou in the adventure called reading.

Harry James Dewberry (13)
Dame Alice Owen's School, Potters Bar

I AM READY

I am ready.
I'm ready to flee.
I'm ready to fly.
I'm ready to hide.
I'm ready to drive.
I'm ready for life to begin.
I am ready.

Elly Sturmy (12)
Dame Alice Owen's School, Potters Bar

SEASONS

Spring

Daisies and buttercups blooming
among all the other flowers,

Sunflowers growing higher than
towers,

Children frolic on the grass,
Whilst the parents chatter allowing
Springtime to pass.

Summer

Summer, summer,
It's almost here,
Time for fun and swimming gear.

Ice cream dripping down my hand.
As the sun blazes on the playing band,

Everyone's happy and getting along,
As we play games,
Like catch and ping-pong.

Autumn

Orange leaves falling off the
bare trees,

Pushing through the leaves that
pile higher than my knees,

Prickly conkers
Falling and popping
Branches snap
Acorns falling.

Winter

Winter is cold with hot
chocolate and sleds,

It's warm and snuggly
when you get into bed,

Snowmen stand tall and
proud
Everyone's laughing and
happy and loud.

Minnie Harris (11)
Greensward Academy, Hockley

A POEM IS JUST THE BEGINNING

A poem is just the beginning
It's never the end of a journey
It's just the start of literature
For many years growing

A new beginning is everywhere
In the world and in the galaxy
New discoveries every day
Beyond our colourful eyes

A new life is a beginning
For animals and people
Objects start speaking
New sentences every day

A new product is produced every day
Like a book, pen or ruler
For you to write wonders,
Poems, stories every day

A new month is just happening
Spring, autumn, summer, winter
So I can write new verses
About everything around me

A poem is just the beginning
It's never the end of a journey
It's just the start of literature
For many years growing

A poem is just the beginning.

Charlotte Wallace (11)
Greensward Academy, Hockley

A POEM IS JUST THE BEGINNING

Peeking through the clouds,
High in the sky,
A tiny bright light,
So sneaky and sly.

Beaming down on Earth,
So bright you couldn't see,
I was soon to find,
My shadow following me.

The clouds disappeared,
The sky so blue and clear,
And the world seemed so peaceful,
Nature was all you could hear.

Hours passed by,
The day was coming to an end,
The sky started to darken,
And the sun started to descend.

The world was now dark,
The sun had gone to bed,
I couldn't help but see,
The stars above my head.

The night sky was pleasant,
And the street lamps flickered,
The world was now asleep,
As the stars shimmered.

Alarna Baker (11)
Greensward Academy, Hockley

WHO IS THAT?

He spots me,
Dark eyes stare,
Looking straight up into mine,
Glistening in the sun.

Paws pad,
Making his way,
His way towards me,
Tail wagging all the while.

Curly hair,
As black as coal,
Silky and fluffy too.

He runs towards me,
Bone in mouth,
Sprinting towards me,
Like a bullet.

The fun we've had,
The games we've played.

He was my lovable puppy,
Coming to say hello!

Evie Hilliard-Fisher (12)
Greensward Academy, Hockley

CATS ARE EVERYWHERE

Cats are everywhere, anywhere, always there,
Even in the . . .
Wool of your socks to the hinges of your doors,
The paint on your walls to the carpets on your floors,
Cats will be there, might you check now to see where cats can be.

Cats are everywhere, anywhere, always there,
Even in the . . .
Feathers in your cushions, the hands on your clocks,
The ink in your pen to the keys in your locks,
Cats will be there, might you check now to see where cats can be.

Cats are everywhere, anywhere, always there,
Even in the . . .
Mud in the ground, to the wood in your gate,
The water in our glass to the food on your plate,
Cats will be there, might you check now to see where cats can be.

Cats are everywhere, anywhere, always there,
Even in the . . .
Clouds in the sky to the leaves on the tree.
The words in a book to your cup of tea,
All these things are only a little of the places your pet cat has been!
But dogs, don't get me started.

Claudia Pergande (11)
Greensward Academy, Hockley

A POEM IS ONLY THE BEGINNING

The polar bear walking softly on the crystal snow,
Yet without a thought or care he wanders there.
To catch a seal, all for the cubs,
She now drifts slowly to a splinter of ice
Through the oil black sea.
For after dark no one dares to mess with the polar bears.

Oliver Nicks (12)
Greensward Academy, Hockley

A POEM IS JUST THE BEGINNING

Her smile reaches up her cheeks
Her legs adorned with beads,
And if you stare into her eyes,
They're bluer than the bluest seas.

A dress of pink and silver,
Shimmering when she sings,
Now hear the bells at her feet,
They ring with the softest of rings.

Glittering sequins embellish her hair,
Sewed on her dress – six flowers,
And in the kindest of her hearts,
She hold a lot of power.

This poem is not the biggest,
But it's just to say she's bold,
She'll stand up for anyone,
She has a heart of gold.

'She' is the person who gives me hope;
Stays with me till the end,
This person I'm talking about,
Is my best friend!

Laura Smiles
Greensward Academy, Hockley

A POEM IS JUST THE BEGINNING

P oems are beautiful pieces of writing, sometimes happy and sometimes romantic.
O nerous as it is at times for the composer it brings joy to those who read their masterpiece.
E veryone is welcome to the journey from composer to reader to enjoy the poem.
M agical is only one of the few words suitable to describe the amazing poem!

Matteo Aylott (11)
Greensward Academy, Hockley

IMAGINE A DIFFERENT WORLD

Imagine a different world,
Where everyone had peace, love and hope,
Where no one worried and panicked,
And everyone was good.

Imagine a different world,
Where war didn't exist,
Bad things didn't happen to good people,
And no one lived in hatred.

Imagine a different world,
Where world hunger didn't haunt us,
Every child was cared for and loved,
Where everyone was as fortunate as we are.

Imagine a different world.
Actually don't,
Though the world has a few flaws,
So do we.

Don't imagine a different world.

Bethany Carlow (11)
Greensward Academy, Hockley

LOVE IS A FEELING

Love is a feeling
Which changes with time,
But, this won't
Happen with me,
Because your love
Is like my life.
It is my world and ecstasy.
I love you for
What you are,
Please don't ever go far
Because I love you a lot!

Kayleigh Barrett (11)
Greensward Academy, Hockley

WINTER

The snow blankets the trees,
The snow drifts in the breeze,
The leaves bejewelled with frost,
The leaves shiny and glossed.

The leaves crunched underfoot,
The snow covered every square-foot,
Rosy cheeked, we try to keep warm,
Along is coming a very large storm.

Pulling woollen hats over our ears,
We go out to play with our peers,
Teeth chatter and cold seeps into our gloves,
As it numbs our fingers in a way that nobody loves.

Winter trees shiver in the bitter wind,
Their branches are all bendy and thinned,
Clusters of twigs, gnarled and twisted,
In the howling wind the flakes drifted.

Beth Rawlings (11)
Greensward Academy, Hockley

A RUGBY POEM

We stand together, muddy, cold, wet in the rain.
The ball is kicked, it's the last play of the game;
Fumbled, it slips to the floor.
I charge at the opposition and pick up the ball.

I gain speed and drop my shoulder;
I smash into a player, who curls up like a boulder.
Not losing pace, mud flies off my boots;
I hit another player . . . *boom!*

The try line's in sight; I dodge a few tackles,
I charge on, the opponent's a shambles.
There's nothing in front of me, apart from the line;
I dive and smash the ball to the ground . . . the try is mine.

Noah Denton (11)
Greensward Academy, Hockley

AUTUMN POEM

Autumn trees
Shed their stunning leaves
Red, yellow, orange, brown
Cascading down.

Cackle, cackle,
Witches brew their magic
Pumpkins carved, sweets galore
Cauldrons bubble.

Whizz, bang
Guy Fawkes' gunpowder plot
The sky is alight
Colours bright.

Autumn goes
Winter sneakily creeps in
Jack Frost comes alive
Winter's here!

Hannah Bibby (11)
Greensward Academy, Hockley

SHARKS

The magnificent Great White,
What a sight,
We should not fear,
As they rarely come near.

To see it catch its prey,
It leaps with its catch of the day,
The theme reminds me every time,
Of the Great White in all its prime.

Sharks are intelligent creatures,
It's a shame they can't teach us,
We could learn from their ways,
As they swim beneath the waves.

Logan Miller (11)
Greensward Academy, Hockley

IN THIS CREEPY GHOST TOWN

I run away from the ghost and hide,
But he says he will be my guide,
In this creepy ghost town.

He shows me all the ghostly gore.
Then he says there is no more.
In this creepy ghost town.

He laced his bony fingers through mine,
As he drank some red blood wine.
In this creepy ghost town.

He takes me to his scary house,
Where nothing lives, not a mouse,
In this creepy ghost town.

Usually, at dinner time we eat corpses.
But especially today, you're our main courses!
In this creepy ghost town.

Beatrix Pattenden (11)
Greensward Academy, Hockley

SEASONS

Bug in the blossoms,
Resurrected in sunlight,
With the pink petals.

Basking in the sun,
Birds sing majestic melodies,
As bright flowers rise.

Colourful trees:
The carpet of orange falls,
Then the frost begins.

Icy branches glow,
Robins sing their sweet song,
Frosty daggers fall.

Nathan Player (11)
Greensward Academy, Hockley

A BEAUTIFUL DAY

As the sun shines bright
It feels so new,
There's not a cloud today
Just a sky of blue.

No breeze to blow
The trees so green
Kites in the sky to be seen
Little bees buzzing,
Working for their queen.

Flowers so colourful and bold
Airing their scents
Blue birds chirping
Sitting on a fence.
What a beautiful day.

Maddie Collins (11)
Greensward Academy, Hockley

A POEM IS JUST THE BEGINNING . . .

My mum gives me more than her eyes,
Her hair and her nose,
She gives me the strength to do what I love,
And her soft hands guide me along.

She lets me go my own way in life,
But she helps a lot of the time,
She spoils me with lots of presents and chocs
But she only wants the best for me.

Yes this poem might not be long,
Yes, it might be boring,
I looked back at all she had done,
And I am happy that she is my mum!

Katie Slaughter (11)
Greensward Academy, Hockley

THE LONE WOLF

Up on the hill
The lone wolf sings
A tune of sorrow
Softly rings
From the tallest mountains
To the lowest valleys
The lone wolf's there
With his mournful cries
The lone wolf
Will sing all day
Be it day or night
He'll give you a fright
The lone wolf will never
Be out of sight.

Flinn Cattanach Ashdown (12)
Greensward Academy, Hockley

AUTUMN

Everything is silent,
Everything but the faint whisper from the cool wind.
As I step outside,
The autumn leaves slowly blow onto my bare face.
Leaving me to steadily peel off the thin moist shapes.

The sun is like a fresh flame burning from afar,
A flame so red and bright it blinds my eyes.
The air was crisp,
And the beautiful brown leaves were falling.
It was a flawless painting hung in a museum.

Although it was perfect now, it would soon all change,
The picturesque scene would soon become a desolate land of snow.
But for this moment it was stunning!

Elizabeth Potter (12)
Greensward Academy, Hockley

STORM MONSTER

Slowly, but surely, charcoal clouds roll towards the innocent city.
Small, icy water droplets appear from the dark sky.
The storm monster has arrived.
Suddenly rain starts tipping down.
Citizens try hard not to drown.
'A monsoon! A monsoon!' people shout.
The crystal water bounces off coats,
As everybody tries to stay afloat,
Shouts and screams pierce the night,
Birds frantically take flight.
When will this nightmare ever end?
No one knows.
But they sure hope soon . . .

Genevieve Booth (11)
Greensward Academy, Hockley

A POEM IS JUST THE BEGINNING

The creatures in the wildlife,
The large who sneak into the deep,
The small who make everyone come to life,
And then there's the busy who go to sleep.

Then there's the sea creatures,
The small who sneak high above the deep,
The large who have the best features,
Then there's the hunters who like to leap.

Then there's the insects,
The small who tend to bite,
Then there's the annoying crickets,
Then there's the large who like to fight.

Jacob Wardle (11)
Greensward Academy, Hockley

DEATH

The dead, the dead
Corpses stained crimson red
The field ridden with crows
Nervous soldiers stand in rows
Shoulder to shoulder, barrels at aim
Trust me, death is not a video game
Death is pain, death is rain
Nothing you shall gain by calling it a game
Death is not for the vain.

The thunder struck hard
Fiendish demons stand guard
Their hides thick and barred
Patiently waiting to take an innocent life
But no one is innocent,
You've all used a knife
This poem may be strange
But that's the point:
If you didn't think it's strange
You're really quite deranged.

Sam Fenwick
Greensward Academy, Hockley

EVOLUTION

I have watched mankind evolve
Building away at their little refuge
All so plain but unique.
I know . . . I'll come back in a week.
I gaze upon what they have built
That boat has made their day
But wait . . . I will return in a century
I find out what became of their mind
War broke out, what do I do?
People dying, what are they doing?
But I can't change it.
I must leave then return
What . . . what happened?
Money, a home and a life, they have done it
They made an important change
I will return.
Falling into a dream
I noticed they didn't need me
I can't control them, I can only watch
I can't return if they don't need me
Goodbye Mankind . . . Goodbye!

Raffaele Marra (12)
Hertswood Academy, Borehamwood

O SUMMER

O summer, O summer
You come in July
The sun shines out so children smile
Ice lollies out, tongues look blue
Children's giggles help us fly.

O summer, O summer
Flowers come out, so do the bees
Help me now!
Roses, tulips, sunflowers
Climb up high, only to touch the sun to own some pride.

O summer, O summer
Where did you go?
I need you here
I need you now.

O summer, O summer
I might just die
I need some tissues
Or I might just cry.

Habibah Islam (12)
Hertswood Academy, Borehamwood

THE NEED TO SLEEP

(Lipogram – I)

Darkness engulfs the world, yet darkness doesn't engulf me,
Thoughts swell through my head, the need to flee.
Events of the day replay over and over,
As though the world gets slower and slower.

Embarrassments of the day before,
Overwhelm me, they make me feel sore.
Hopefully embarrassment doesn't occur anew,
But that only happens to a few.

Blameless, pure words taken gravely,
Arguments start, others end sharply.
Bonds are key to contentment,
Else you'll come across resentment.

However, we forgot to ponder on moments of joy,
When we used to play and cry, 'Ahoy!'
When our bonds are always there for us
When they help make a memory for us.

Yet the future lay ahead,
Old events we put to bed.
New starts to make are around the corner
New thoughts to have through my head.

My eyes slowly start to become weary,
Burnout must be my theory.
The smell of the sheets overcomes me,
As natural as a tree.

Darkness engulfs the world and darkness may engulf me,
Thoughts swell through my head, the need to sleep.
Peaceful thoughts run over and over,
Guess here's my chance to sleep deeper and deeper.

Joanna Armistead (14)
Hertswood Academy, Borehamwood

ADRENALINE

(Lipogram – U)

Her deepest desires, all tamed when it's immense yet vehement
The inside chemical reactions perform like fireworks
The existence of it feels almost like her own creation in which she only knows
With every word spoken, enlightenment hits her.

Polished, legendary.

A hypothetical location filled with forgotten memories and acceptance
What is more masterly than a non-fictional image from an invisible world?
She's walking, walking down her devised path with it in her ears.
Socialisation has vanished from every depth of her remembrance.

Wandering in her personal maze of resonance.

Connected with her inner peace, finally she can breathe.
It is her obsession yet not even a physical entity
If only they knew how deeply this really goes.

However they can't, as when they listen all they hear
Is simply another annoying song.

Jessica Bruce
Hertswood Academy, Borehamwood

RED IS EVERYWHERE

Red is like a fire engine, quick and speedy,
Also looks like blood and shines like a ruby,
Red can mean anger or danger,
Or can mean love and roses,
Red is like fire and flames,
Also can look lovely when sunrise comes,
Hundreds of people look every morning,
Red is everywhere.

Daisy Elicia Ferozha-Warwick (12)
Hertswood Academy, Borehamwood

O WINTER

O winter, O winter
The festive time
The colour of the snow reflects on the sky.

O winter, O winter
The frosty trees
The summer's gone with the bees.

O winter, O winter
Children enjoying their weeks off school
Building snowmen, throwing snow,
This is how the winter time goes.

Kira Reed (12)
Hertswood Academy, Borehamwood

EFFORT TURNED TO NOTHING

Injuries, stress, illness.
The feeling you get from seeing your friends on the pitch,
Witnessing from the bench, completely helpless.
It silently tormenting you,
Nothing you do will help,
The worry there is to show the loneliness you feel
Terrified of distressing others – letting them down.
You don't expect them to recognise,
Indeed you just want to frown.
Just observing whilst everyone begins to split,
Defence slowly crumbling, strikers outshine.
You know you should be out there, do they even know you left?
Your kit, your position, your number
Given on whilst you're gone.
Countless doctors visits, how did things go so wrong?
Consistently questioning if you'll ever get to return
You never get the simple response, just the pity.
Soreness, discomfort, suffering
Your effort turned to nothing.

Morgan-Paige Basham
Hertswood Academy, Borehamwood

CRIMSON – WHAT COULD IT SHOW?

Crimson is a stunning colour, but could be sinful.
It is a colour full of passion.
Crimson is part of autumn's fashion.
It shows up in humans dying
And flying to bliss
Following a sad, tiny kiss.
A crimson poppy of past wars shows us that.
Crimson is a drop of blood which is scary and full of horror
Crimson is a colour full of conflict.
It is odd,
Crimson shows all this. Full stop!

David Delia (12)
Hertswood Academy, Borehamwood

THE SAVANNAH

The savannah is a place full of wildlife,
Which the infants wish to experience
Wild tigers and cheetahs run after their prey,
Like athletes in the swishing dry grass.
Elephants fight to survive in the burning heat,
Travelling days and days searching after water.
When they find it they suck it up with their trunks,
Like a vacuum cleaner.
Meerkats scavenge everywhere after ant nests
Like buyers glancing after brilliant deals
There are giraffes that chew leaves as if they are large pieces of bubblegum.
But, besides that, there are much sadder parts
In which all living things in the savannah fade away.
Such as animals killing different animals
I belive when it is the right time we will all return back as animals,
Even if it means we aren't animals in the savannah.

Savannah Endean (12)
Hertswood Academy, Borehamwood

SUMMER BREEZE

Summer is a lovely season,
Everyone enjoys it, there's a very good reason.
I love going shopping to get all the new trends,
So much to buy, the packing never ends.
We are all ready to get on the plane,
Excitement is building, no more rain.

My relatives and I love swimming in the sea,
Lovely soft sand as warm as can be.
I'm laying on the beach, getting a tan,
We cool ourselves down with a nice cold can.
Later we all go and get an ice cream,
This is the best holiday ever, it's just like a dream.

Becky Leech (12)
Hertswood Academy, Borehamwood

MY GRANDMA

(Lipogram – I)

She's my world, my grandma,
Worth more to me than all the world's gold.
Every word that comes out of her mouth comes out warm and gentle.
Her soul's full of love and laughter,
Her laugh warms the heart of all.
When she loves someone, the love comes from her golden heart,
Valuable and strong.
She's someone who has walked my ways,
Someone who knows my every need.
At moments when she would see me cry,
She would mop my tears and her heart would nearly bleed
She has the tenderness of a mother
My heart wants my grandma to be there and watch me grow,
Though she's at a country, far away
Her heart's adjacent to my heart.

Matilda Shkupi
Hertswood Academy, Borehamwood

THE WOLVES

Across the snow they creep,
Through the meadows they sneak,
Caves are where wolves sleep,
Shadows are where they stay.
Across the valleys they go,
They pass through the forest to go home,
They chase the deer across the meadows,
And down to the woods.
They howl at the moon for fun,
And nap under the sun.
Across the snowy valley they go,
Back to the cave where they sleep.

Kerri-Anne Morris (12)
Hertswood Academy, Borehamwood

UNTITLED

Joyful or gloomy, we need it,
Quick or slow, we need it,
We need to move,
We need to jig,
Listen so much we bleed it.

Different lingo, we love it,
Different genre, we love it,
We lose ourselves,
We find ourselves,
Listen so much, we rise above it.

It surrounds us,
Engulfs us,
So good it's impossible to sit.
Inspires us, influences us,
To be honest, we couldn't live without it.

Ellen Tester (14)
Hertswood Academy, Borehamwood

O FOOTBALL, O FOOTBALL

(Lipogram – I)

O, football, O, football where do we start?
Each player's talented, each has a part
The tackles hurt but we cannot stop
When he runs around the players and he takes the shot.
The manager yells to 'take them out!'
But the referee screams and shouts
The cards are shown, the spectators hate
The other team starts to celebrate
When the ball gets shot and reaches the net
The people start to place a bet
The cup needs to be won
But only by one
So, well done boys, we have won!

Alfie Basham (12)
Hertswood Academy, Borehamwood

WHAT'S UP THERE?

(Lipogram – I)

Has anyone ever told you the sky's where your dreams come true?
Maybe so, but have you ever looked beyond the sky?
There are many creatures and planets up there.
Mars, the red planet where there are volcanos larger than Everest.
Also the moon's up there;
Everybody used to say the moon was made of cheese
But the moon can be made of whatever you please
Stars can be good
When you're lost they take you home
Black holes may be scary
But when you go through you open up a new part of your soul
To go through a black hole can be the same as the start of school
You're scared, but after, you're cool
Remember space can make your dreams come true!

Lucas Gannon (12)
Hertswood Academy, Borehamwood

CAMERAS

Cameras surround me like a spy on a mission.
I've tried to write about how uncomfortable I feel with these cameras in these positions.
From your front room to your bedroom, my concern begins to grow.
It seems my letters to the dictator are neglected and not shown.

However, there's a knock at my door
The thought entered my head: the dictator had read my letters for sure.
And it was ...

Changes were made as if the world was a different place.
My mind was finally relaxed
Not to be followed all the time, without them leaving a trace.
My life feels like I have my own space.
Now these cameras are gone, I now feel safe.

Belle Shannon
Hertswood Academy, Borehamwood

SHARK, OCEAN'S DEVIL FISH

Across oceans worldwide,
I swim close, by your side.
A cunning weapon from seas I am.
Feared by all, especially man.
And so I never sleep,
As I reign over seas deep.

I have been ruling seas since dinosaurs roamed around land,
I can lurk in clear oceans or in murky liquid near sand.
Forged millions of years ago,
By an evil demon from below.
I conquered seas since world's prime,
Now I swim freely; all seas are mine.

Who will end my reign of fear?
No one, you will never know when I appear.

Tajbir Singh
Hertswood Academy, Borehamwood

TO BE IN LOVE

(Lipogram – C)

Veins flowing, blood pumping,
All I saw was red,
Heartbreaking, painstaking,
I wanted to be dead.

Tears falling, I was bawling,
He was in my head,
Memories made, the bruises fade,
My heart now heavier than lead.

Body hurting, eyes burning,
I had a sensation of dread,
No more noise, no more boys,
I bled and bled and bled.

Holly Graber (14)
Hertswood Academy, Borehamwood

LOVE STORY

The story of us started off so great,
I knew all too well it's one that would break,
I know you're not sorry for everything you've done,
I regret our last kiss, the hugs and the laughs.
Our love was a one-way ticket to sorrow,
Now I see red when I think of you.

It used to feel sweeter than fiction,
Like our own wonderland,
You ruined that once innocent girl,
But now I can be fearless and stronger than ever,
This love is good, this love is bad.

Christina Angus
Hertswood Academy, Borehamwood

ANIMALS

Cats and dogs
Fish and frogs
All so amazing
Cows a-grazing
Goats and kids
Lions and cubs
And itsy, bitsy tiny grubs
All God's living things
Things that sting and things with wings

So strong, so small, so short, so tall,
So amazingly fabulous, all in all.

Lauren Holmes
Hertswood Academy, Borehamwood

SUMMER'S DAY

I love a summer's day,
Sun blazing, wind swaying,
A rainbow occurs, wonderful and full of colours,
Have you ever wondered if a pile of gold is relaxing
At the end of the rainbow?
Wildlife comes, crawling around, hiding away,
Oh, how I love a summer's day,
A range of colours, way up high
And the smell of my mum's apple pie,
I hear a call, I wish I can remain, speak again one day,
I'll miss you, my summer's day.

Paige Shadbolt (12)
Hertswood Academy, Borehamwood

LEAVES

(Lipogram – F)

How silently they tumble down,
And come to rest upon the ground,
Beneath the trees without a care.

At other times, they wildly glide,
Until they reach the sky with pride,
Twisting through the air.

They are all exhausted,
And drop down to the Earth below.

Bleon Shalaku
Hertswood Academy, Borehamwood

NATURE

Nature is an amazing thing
Where hidden secrets can be detected
Like the way the sun is reflected
It's beautiful the way it increases largely in size
The way in which the bees are flying high and freely
The way infants wish to explore new adventures
Seeing squirrels sneakily salvaging in the swaying trees
Spiders crawling and lurking for prey
Berries getting bigger every day
The way in which the trees swish in the gentle breeze.

Hayley-Jade John (12)
Hertswood Academy, Borehamwood

YOU

(Lipogram – S)

Love or hope, a word from above,
Pure and clean, a metaphoric dove.
Don't worry, an untethered endeavour,
Forever, a quiet time when we're together.

Heighten our perception, impact the blow,
Creating a menace, life to and fro.
Forgiving a luxury one cannot maintain,
But I'd rather try than live my life in vain.

Levi Kane (14)
Hertswood Academy, Borehamwood

A MESSAGE IN A BOTTLE

Dear God,

My husband told me that we were going soon
'To ride the waves of freedom,' he'll declare
He'll tie the knot and hang us with his noose,
Behind the gossamers of his despair.

My husband told me that the waves are warm,
Hospitable, in every hiss and bite;
He'll whip our flesh until it's ripped and worn,
He can't subdue the will of fate's insight.

My husband told me that we'll all be fine,
To fall to the romantic lure of the sea,
He'll just repeat that old, euphonic line.
Now death welcomes its new companions. Three.

O God, please save my husband and have his grief undone,
And let me offer up my body, if you'll please just spare my son!

Yours sincerely.

Sabrina Miller (15)
Immanuel College School, Bushey

LOVE

Where friendships are made,
And memories cherished,
When dreams come true,
And family new,
Nothing could be stronger,
Than the bond between you and another.

You treasure the moments when you are together,
Hoping that it will last forever,
Laugh, giggle and be free,
All you think is you and me,
Boys, girls side by side,
Always there when you need to hide.

From sitting in the assembly hall,
To going shopping in the mall,
Staring romantically at each other,
Getting told off by your mother,
Can't help but text one more time,
Knowing that he is mine.

Wearing his comfy baggy clothes,
Everyone needs some of those,
Going out on cute first dates,
Leaving without your best mates,
All is going oh so well,
Until it all turns to hell.

Your dreams are through
Evenings spent without you know who,
Sitting crying up to the moon,
They all say you'll get over him soon,
At first he was the only one,
But now he is simply another one.

Lucy Packman (13)
Kings Langley School, Kings Langley

MONTHS

January's weather is awfully bleak,
We resist to step outside to take a peek.

February is a dark, gloomy grey,
No sight of brilliant rays.

March invites birds humming,
We know that spring is slowly approaching.

April brings the Easter Bunny,
Chocolate melting because it's sunny.

May delivers flowers in full bloom,
And it will be bright very, very soon.

June presents long cheery days,
Not long now 'til we're in a summer haze.

July brings a spat of sun cream,
No scarves or hats anywhere to be seen.

August is bright and brings no glum,
This is the month that always stays fun.

September is the month for summertime blues,
Back to work and the routine resumes.

October sees golden leaves fall from trees,
Lit pumpkins and witches' cackles float on the breeze.

November remember the 5th of November,
The fireworks display is a sight to remember.

December twinkles like sparkling stars,
Snowflakes start to drift from afar.

Rosanna Rushton (12)
Kings Langley School, Kings Langley

BELOVED

Receive me
For I offer my body and soul
To your sagacious disposition.

My willing heart
Docile to your solicits
My fidelity exceeds those that claim love for you
Because I am yours – only yours.

Bond me
Use your soul to confine me
Don't use your hands
For they are just the redundance
Of your anatomy.

Your mind is what I require.

Let us combine but
Not in holy matrimony
For no paper or ring could
Define the infatuation that
Has blossomed within our intellect.

Don't doubt me
My love is reliable.
If my body fails
My soul will remain
Its vehement atrocities.
For I am me and will only be the imperfect me.

Flaw against flaw, we create the epitome of perfection.

Robyn Stevenson (13)
Kings Langley School, Kings Langley

AUTUMN

The invigorating walk with the dogs,
Crisp air flowing through my hair.
It's making me think Christmas is nearly here.

Silky, smooth hot chocolate,
Deliciously indulgent,
Soaking down my throat,
Like a sponge soaking up water, instantly rehydrating.

Wellies back in fashion,
With leaves collapsing under their weight,
Cracking and crumbling like a firework,
Exploding into thousands of sprinkles of joy.

Sparklers being swung round and round,
They are little baby bonfires blooming.
When I look outside all I see,
Is leaves falling from the tree.
Their colours, the fire ashes burning into nothing.

But...
There's another side to autumn which others see,
Blooming flowers becoming lifeless,
With the stern touch and hard stare of autumn
Digging into the flower's pollen heart.

Making the bees buzz away,
The squirrels leaving their summer holidays,
And approaching their deep sleep.
Everyone's settling down to a cold autumn night.

Beth Edwards (12)
Kings Langley School, Kings Langley

MOUNTAIN HEAVEN

Like a wise old man,
Staring down on people,
With old frosty, white hair.
Trees guarding all around,
Nothing getting through.

Climbing, legs aching, getting higher,
Two steps forward, one step back.
Breathing in fresh, sweet air.

Silence, calm silence,
Calm, peaceful silence
Hearing the beat of my heart.
Looking around, impressed,
Surrounded by soft, light air.

A crown of snow rests on top.
Whistling wind in one ear,
Out the other
Misty, cold.

Feeling higher than the stars,
Wide and free.
Troops following the leader
Reaching the top.

Digging into a slice of heaven, mountain heaven.

Bethany Howard (13)
Kings Langley School, Kings Langley

SEASONS

In winter the sweet singing birds are gone.
Some flew to Africa and beyond.
The country turned white.
As the winds gush, blast and bite.
Ground so deep with snow, slush and sleet.
I hate the feeling when you can't feel your frozen feet.

In spring, fields are full of flowers and life
Setting the seeds in the fields of sun,
The animals come out to have some fun.
I think it's time to dance and sing,
To celebrate the beauty of spring.

In summer, the world is alive,
Bees are buzzing – getting food to the hive.
You may catch me snoozing in the grass,
Harvesting crops the colour of brass.

In Autumn the crisp leaves fall down with a whirl,
You wake in the morning to a foggy mist.
Now it's time to say bye to the warm coloured autumn
And hello to the vast winter.

Megan Goodall (13)
Kings Langley School, Kings Langley

THE GIRL IN THE BACK

There's a girl in black
Her pale face and ebony hair stands out from the crowd.

She's silent and doesn't seem to try or joke.
She's not perplexed about the people sniggering and staring over her.

Her lips are valiant and her face glimmers like gold
She's eager to learn and her face is stern.
She never makes conversation – however, she's always heard.

She's just a girl in black,
With a pale face and ebony hair.

But inside she's fighting a battle for acceptance
She wants to be acknowledged but

She's just a girl in black
With a pale face and ebony hair.

She wants to make conversation
Stop people from staring
Be accepted and speak her mind.

Holly Bradshaw (12)
Kings Langley School, Kings Langley

MCLAREN P1

Red, orange, black, white, green and blue
You can race or you can cruise

Engine rips and roars
Faster than a cheetah, faster than lightning
With speed that is nail biting

Leather seats to sink in
Smooth and soft fabrics
Connected with precision stitching
The steering wheel, seats and doors.

100, 200, 300 miles per hour
Back wing unfolds as you put your foot down

Like an animal the engine roars
It's no car, it's a beast!

Jack Hancock (13)
Kings Langley School, Kings Langley

STOCK CAR RACING

I love to go stock car racing
It is always amazing
You get really dirty
And it can get frustrating.

Racing is so entertaining
I will never miss a meeting
It is real fun, even when it's raining

Building the cars is just the beginning
Breaking, cutting, ripping and smashing
You end up saving some of it.

Then it comes to racing – it is always chaos
After the race there is nothing left
Might as well scrap it.

Danny McCarthy (13)
Kings Langley School, Kings Langley

US

Our light, encased by wonders and mysteries,
Fighting back darkness that could swallow us whole.
A disease caused by the unknown,
Making our hands dirty with all the dire things,
Our once innocent minds thought that our hands acted against.

It's us that stands between the light and oblivion.
The fire in our soul keeps us,
Sometimes it gets too hard to control.
Others think it's OK putting this fire out,
But aren't they only putting out theirs?

Why does darkness scare us?
Should whatever lurks in it frighten us?
Their own abyss embedded within us
Is one of the biggest fears shaped in us?

Our light is what 'it' envies the most,
The dear most precious thing in our essence.
However little by little,
It gets the better of us.
Devouring us.
Killing us.
Yet we don't realise

Don't disappear into the night,
Danger lies ahead.
Whirring, crashing, thudding
Could be the last things you hear.
When it's too late don't come calling back,
Because we're the victim it wanted the most,
Us.

Shenelle Davis
Marriotts School, Stevenage

PYROPHOBIA

Suddenly the fun all stopped as he froze like a statue,
The show had been spectacular and he had loved it
Until they came, the men with devils' sticks.
They were spun as though engulfing the performers in a force field
The light radiating off was astounding.
He couldn't bear it though,
He began to run,
Running, running, running,
Never looking back.
Finally he reached a clearing,
In the crystal moonlight
I finally saw it, the fear in his eyes.
He sat down on a log and began to cry,
What could have happened?
Was he hurt?
I approached him cautiously . . .
'Son, what's wrong?'
'The fire,' he said, 'it was all around me'
'It was spectacular wasn't it?'
'No it wasn't actually'
And then it hit me
He was in fear.

Harry Welham (13)
Marriotts School, Stevenage

LIGHT

Light fills the sky at the stroke of the clock,
The night falls at the blinding sight.
Colours returned to the Earth in just one tick,
From deep inside delicate soil to as tall as sky high,
You never know what seeks in the light's eye.

The first light that flashes in your eyes,
Is the start of a brand new life.
The first star you see is out of billions to find,
However far you seek, however far you look,
You never know what seeks in the light's eye.

The wonderful colours of the world,
Are just little tweaks of emotions to your world,
There are so many ranges of colours to emotions,
Can you ever have enough colours without light?
You never know what seeks in the light's eye.

Light is what you need when you are afraid,
Scared of what the darkness can lead to.
The light feels reassuring,
It gives warmth and sometimes love,
But you never know what seeks in the light's eye.

Tess Xiao (12)
Marriotts School, Stevenage

WHERE HAS YOUR LIGHT GONE?

The electricity is flickering
The light is disappearing
But the future is looking bright

Reach for the stars in the deathly night
Matchsticks striking, lantern flying
Happiness in the word that appears in sight
Fireworks exploding in the ebony sky

A shiver of warmth runs down my spine
The glistening moon in the Halloween night
A glaze of heat hits my face
The world is one fiery place

The sun is rising
The night has gone
You may think this is the end but it's just the start
Come back at midnight
When the light will spark.

Maddison Malocco (11)
Marriotts School, Stevenage

LIGHT IS MY KNIGHT

When I think of light I think of hope,
Carefully always makes me cope.

The light makes me not think about the scary night,
The light is my knight.

The light drives me like a car,
It always gets me far.

Light is my helper,
It is my warm shelter.

Carmel Corpe (11)
Marriotts School, Stevenage

UNTITLED

The night is like the light,
But only I think it's not.
Why?
I ask you why?
Why are we living like this?
Like a rat running through dark,
We are like the animals
That live in the barn, why?
Why are we living?
Why are we here?
Why?
Why I ask you?
Why? Just let me know
Why?
It's all just a big lie.

Ellie Price (12)
Marriotts School, Stevenage

HONEY YOU LIGHT UP MY DAY

Honey you light up my day
You always know what to say
You are my light source to my heart
I'm depressed when we're apart
Honey you light up my day
You're my prince, I'm your princess
I'm your shining star and you're my beautiful sky
You're my smile, I'm your laughter
Honey you light up my day.
When it's a hot summer's evening
We stay in and watch a movie
But when it's time to dance you get groovy
After work you always get looney (in a good way)
So this is why you light up my day.

Rosie-Mae Blackie (11)
Marriotts School, Stevenage

LIGHT

Light is like life, it goes on and off,
Light illuminates the darkness,
Light is a baby's smile,
But light is the one that guides the way,
And brings all things together.
Light will never leave because,
You are light and you can,
Shine bright all though the night,
Light,
Light,
Is a wonderful thing,
Light,
Light,
Is where all happiness begins.

Courtney Daly (11)
Marriotts School, Stevenage

SCHOOL

S chool is boring most of the time
C ome on people, you're wasting your time
H ow can we do all of the homework?
O nly the smart can do all the classwork
O ut of the doors at 3:20
L et's go home, we've done plenty.

Michael Archer (14)
Passmores Academy, Harlow

THE DAY GETS BRIGHTER

Just because
people
laugh
joke
and smile
doesn't mean to say
they'll be here for a
while

Because
at the end of the day
when they return home
and the fake smile
drops
they open up the
tissue box
and out come the
tears
she's been holding in
for years

But
in the morning
when she opens
the door
her friends
come along
and make
her day
so much brighter

She no longer has
to pretend
as all the sadness
comes to an end
because of the
support of her
amazing friends

Never let anyone
bring their life to

an end
there's nothing you'll
miss more than the
brightest smile
of your bestest friend.

Georgia Moore (14)
Passmores Academy, Harlow

TEENAGE LIFE

Being a teenager is awkward and unfair
Being treated like children
But expected to behave like adults
Being made out to be 'bad'
When really we are mostly good
Thinking we stay on streets smoking and drinking
When we are at home studying for our GCSEs
There is so much pressure
On becoming a teenager
You make out
Our lives depend on our teenage years

Not all of us smoke
Drink
Scare people
Break the law
We are nice people
Why can't you see that?
You pick out the smallest
Most tiniest
Group of us and say we are 'bad'
Well we're not
So please treat us how we act
You make being a teenager
Awkward
And
Unfair.

Mollie Johns (14)
Passmores Academy, Harlow

THE MONSTER WITHIN

This monster resides within me
Drowns my emotions like the sea
I hear it screech and howl and scream
Until down my face the tears start to stream

I have to lie
For it is clouding my mind
I can't hear myself think
But we seem to be in sync

It is slowly taking over my life
I am planning to soon take the knife
And fight this battle like I should
Cut it out of my life for good

The monster resides within me
It's blinding me and I can't see
I am finally becoming it
Or maybe it's become me?

I want to be free
I need to be free
It's consuming me whole
I've now got a broken soul

It feeds on my pain
Making me dull like rain
I can't let my monster win
Yet it's too deep below my skin

I will take it with me
To the grave
Where I'll forever
Be its slave.

Daria Stoszek (14)
Passmores Academy, Harlow

THE POETRY TRIALS - HERTFORDSHIRE & ESSEX

THE ONES

You say you'll always remember
That you'll always have the time
You're never going to forget them
They're always on your mind

But time never stops moving
Posters start to fade
Some day you'll have memories
Of this fandom that was made

In July my life was born
Nobody knows how much you mean
You're the most beautiful boy I have seen
It was an eclipse from the heart
I knew I loved you from the start

Liam really is a 'payne'
Maybe he got some tips off Zayn?
But for now I'll let Niall take the blame
Maybe it was all the fame

They don't understand
They think of them, nothing
More than a band

Niall's obsession with Nando's
Is almost as bad as Harry going commando
He doesn't even care if it's covered in coriander
He'd even eat it from a blender
As long as the chicken is tender
If it is not, he'll show his anger.

Becky Melanie Shaw (14)
Passmores Academy, Harlow

THE MONSTER INSIDE

Sticks and stones may break my bones
But names will permanently lay
The comments continue
You'll never forget the twisted words they say

Each word said
Rests in your head
Restless nights lay ahead
All you desire is sleep
Bags hang from your eyes
A new label, insomniac freak

A whirlpool of pain
A never-ending chain
It's like you're screaming
But no one can hear
Your cry for help
But no one cares my dear

You appear insignificant
When you're actually magnificent
You're unable to look in the mirror
A poor soul afraid of their own reflection
You're too blind to notice the perfection.

That's what happens you see
Because no one can hide
From the monster inside.

Gracey Dorling (14)
Passmores Academy, Harlow

THE MUSICAL

Performing is everything to me
It can really touch you
The more emotion you put in
The stronger the audience feel
The musicals are my favourites
It brings you alive a bit more
The words of a song can have a strong thought against you

The way they act on stage is magnificent
They have these big loud voices
And you can only understand what their words mean
If you listen really carefully.

The dances they do can bring happiness to the eye
When you look really carefully from up above
You can see the expressions they have on their faces
Whilst they're dancing in that spotlight
You know they are having a wonderful time
Trying to make the audience feel as if they are dancing with them

The beautiful music that plays underneath the actor's monologue
Really speaks to you from the heart
They know what they're feeling as they speak
We don't know how this musical will end
But the actors, well they know, they've read the script a thousand times.

Wow! That musical was touching, you were so right.

Claudia Agnes (14)
Passmores Academy, Harlow

CHICKEN

I love KFC
Because it is so tasty

The fries are the best
They make me so tight in the chest
They're better than the rest
KFC is my nest

I also love their Bargain Buckets
What with all the fries and nuggets
Though eating too much makes me sluggish
And I hate disposing of the rubbish

There's nothing like their popcorn chicken
Tastes so good, so finger-licking
And as the clock keeps ticking
I eat more and more chicken

I love to eat their wraps
Though I think they're a trap
Just to make civilians fat

I really need to stop the food
Because I keep burping
I feel so rude
And all my mates keep saying
'Cut out the chicken, dude!'

James Wright (15)
Passmores Academy, Harlow

THE POETRY TRIALS - HERTFORDSHIRE & ESSEX

LOVE

When I was eleven I found a boy
He told me I was the one
But I just turned out to be a fool
My nan told me, 'Don't worry love will come'
But I thought I will never trust someone again
So I decided that music was in my heart
My nan said, 'I can imagine you on X Factor'
Then I got stage fright
And it all started again
I'm in love with a boy
He thinks it's funny
Before my nan died in December 2014
I told her about the boy I'm still in love with
She said, 'Follow your dreams'
And she died, I cried
So I sang on her grave
Then like magic my stage fright disappeared
Now I can picture her saying
'Go girl, you can do it'
I'm not afraid anymore
Love is not a hobby, it's a passion
I miss my nan's voice
Love for me is never-ending
I want real love not the popular kind.

Rianna Samuels (14)
Passmores Academy, Harlow

THEY NEVER SEE

People think I am a goody-two-shoes
But really I always feel blue
They always see the nice side of me
Why can't they just let me be?
Try to keep to yourself
Myself, as I always do.

In school we are a deck of cards
You have the popular cards, kings, queens, Jacks
And then you have the odd ones, the jokers
The cards that nobody likes, the cards that nobody uses
We all get shifted around
Put in places, you don't feel safe and sound

People think I am a goody-two-shoes
But really I always feel blue
They never see the other side of me
As they will not believe
I wish to leave.

They don't know me behind closed doors
They will never know
You get name called, poked fun at
Then you know that in years to come
They won't be happy enough to see the sun.

Kyra Jayne Hiett (14)
Passmores Academy, Harlow

SOCIAL MEDIA

Social media
Where's the social?

What happened
To the world we once had?

No iPhones, iPads, iPods
Where are we?

We once were connected
But that all changed!

Upload after upload
Yet not a single mention

The society we once had
All got thrown away

No communication
Maybe just a tag

Doesn't that seem sad ... ?

What happened to the world we once had?
Don't you miss it?

- Just a tad ...

Shana Barrows (14)
Passmores Academy, Harlow

UNTITLED

It was the night of Halloween
I was going to bed
But I'll never forget
What I saw in my head

The lights were all off
The house was in darkness
My bedroom door opened
And it was all blackness

It was a horror movie
It was like nothing real
The figure in front of me
I could not feel

I hid under my bed
Wishing to die
But all I could do
Was helplessly cry

I thought to myself
What is this hell?
As I slowly pulled down the covers
I thought to myself, *Oh well!*

Kieran Berry (14)
Passmores Academy, Harlow

ZAYN MALIK POEM

Boy can draw
Chiselled jaw
Not a flaw in sight
All he ever wants to do is take a flight

He has now gone solo
A hole through his heart like a Polo
No longer with Perrie
In recent interviews he hasn't been very merry.

Megan Slater (14)
Passmores Academy, Harlow

THE GHOST OF THE LOST BOY

His ghost is still here
He never leaves
He is always near
I remember his sleeves

Blue as the night sky
I remember it so clear
He never wore a tie
I know he is near

I loved him
I won't say I didn't
His little brother Tim
Is going way out of his limits

When he said he was fine
It was strange
Till I found it was a lie
He was in his own cage

Now it's too late
He's gone forever
He changed his fate
I will never feel the same way, *ever!*

Nicole Delanbanque (14)
Passmores Academy, Harlow

FOOTBALL

The ball is played on the pitch
Their number one striker is Mitch
The game kicks off, hopefully they can win
But at the moment they can't hit a bin

They're in their half,
They have the ball
The crowd is cheering
And going mental.

Samuel Cleverdon (14)
Passmores Academy, Harlow

LIFE OF A SWIMMER

Waking up at half 5 to go training
Life of a swimmer

Having your hair smell like chlorine every day
Life of a swimmer

Always hungry
Life of a swimmer

Missing out on social life
Life of a swimmer

Training nine hours a week
Life of a swimmer

Spending every weekend at a swim meet
Life of a swimmer

Not interested in make-up, interested in costumes
Life of a swimmer

Eat, sleep, swim, I'm ready to go to achieve my personal best, off I go!
Life of a swimmer

Swimming is my life!

Emily Hills (15)
Passmores Academy, Harlow

WHAT HAPPENED?

It was as black as it could be, yet as light as it had ever been
The night was as foggy as a white cloud

It happened very fast
It was almost as fast as a fast car

Or maybe I just fainted and then woke up when it was all over
Then I saw a man lying on the floor under the bright yellow light

I don't know what happened
But maybe I will never know.

Skye Perkins (14)
Passmores Academy, Harlow

POEM

You're fat
You're ugly
You're stupid
You're worthless
Society has led you to believe
All these things
Although you have a smile upon your face
On the inside you feel like you're a disgrace
Worries and fears build up in your head
You feel anxious and isolated while lying in bed

You can no longer control
The emotions you feel
On the side you see a blade of steel ...

You are no longer in this world
But society cannot understand
Why someone so perfect
Would do this

Although you feel that stuff was true
It turns out no one can be a better you.

Charlotte May Chiraghuddin (14)
Passmores Academy, Harlow

BULLYING POEM

People get hurt, people get scared
Feeling ripped like paper being teared

As she cries to sleep every night
Clenching her eyelids really tight

Scared to speak, scared to shout
She has no one there, no one about

Feeling alone, feeling isolated
Feeling hurt, feeling underrated.

Brittany Russell (14)
Passmores Academy, Harlow

THE MYSTERIOUS OCEAN

The ocean's one big mystery
It creates a lot of great history
There are so many little things that are unsolved
And there are many bad things that need to be solved
There are many unsolved myths that need to be told
But in order to do that we gotta be brave 'n' bold
Many famous people fought on the ocean
But all this bad fighting brought great emotion
The ocean is one heck of a beautiful place
But we know less about it than we do our own space

Do you really know what's at the bottom of the sea?
Or do you know much more about the dark anatomy?

The ocean's so mysterious just like extraterrestrial life
But when you think of aliens you jump up and thrive
Do you not care what's at the bottom of what surrounds us?
Do you think that the ocean's just one big fuss?

The ocean may give us a breakthrough in life
So why don't you get ready and dive?

Jake Balding (14)
Passmores Academy, Harlow

COLD

I walk out to the freezing cold snow
Wishing that I now know
About what I did, fighting my own actions
Can't stop my reactions
Yet the next day I start thinking that I am the big man
Yet all things start unravelling in my hand
It was a hole in my chest just like a well deep in the ground
The bad things that I did I wish I could have hid
All the accusations flying around
Yet they all are pointed towards my common ground.

Emma Oakes (14)
Passmores Academy, Harlow

CREATURES

In the darkness they hide
For the dark has no light
Their time they cannot bide
They fight the thirst with all their might

They are reborn on a full moon
You cannot dance to their tune
Their tune made by their voices
They cannot control their choices

Their bubbling cauldron is what defines them
Where some take their power from a gem
A black cat is a necessity
But a black hat is a rarity.

Although these creatures scare us
What we must realise
Is that we destroy each other
With all our lies.

Jade Smith (14)
Passmores Academy, Harlow

FOOTBALL

The whistle blew and I got kicked around
I could feel the tension in the football ground
Forty five minutes was the test
The players kicking me at their best

Half-time came, time for a break
The team's frustrated with a headache
The second half started and I'm in the net
I flew in the top corner like a rocket jet

Back in the centre because they just scored
I preferred it better when I was bored
The game finished and the players stood tall
And that's the life of a football!

Jed Harrison (14)
Passmores Academy, Harlow

LONELY SPIRITS

The shadows slowly melting their sorrow
No one can see their pain
For them there's only forever tomorrow
They have nothing else to gain

They lurk around an empty place
No one to listen, no one to care
They only see the same lifeless face
Staring back at them, it's not fair

Their faces blank as stone
Their skin as cold as ice
We know they're all alone
But someone had to pay the price

Eventually they are forgotten
Even the Earth becomes careless
They fall and become broken
And the quiet is then endless.

Isabella Curtis (14)
Passmores Academy, Harlow

LOVE

Love can be bad
But when it's good, it's rad
It can hurt, hurt like a knife
And it controls your life

Love is what you desire
It burns you up like fire
Romance normally ends
But you can always turn to friends

You don't even need a gun
You don't even need a pill
If you ever wanna die
Fall in love and you'll get killed.

Robyn Groom (14)
Passmores Academy, Harlow

THE FOOTBALL

I wait anxiously ready to get kicked around
I can feel the tension throughout the ground
The whistle blew and I was kicked
The player started taking the mick
He kept doing stepovers around me
For that team that player was key
Half-time came and I could finally have a rest
The second half would be a massive test
The score was 0-0 it was a bit dull
I was wailing for them to score a goal!
I finally flew into the top of the net
I was going as fast as a rocket jet
The whistle blew for the last time
I got battered so hard it should have been a crime
Finally I can have a rest
For the next game I'll be at my best.

Jack Grey (14)
Passmores Academy, Harlow

WHAT YOU THINK OF ME

You think I'm a thug,
You think I am a threat,
But how would you know if we haven't even met.
You assume that we're bad,
But you don't see the good,
All you think you see is us wearing hoods.
To tell you the truth some of us are,
They push their luck way over the bar,
You don't realise the damage that is there,
Teenagers are troubled, they need someone to care,
Don't judge because deep inside,
There is something that we all hide,
Next time you see us don't think of us as bad,
Remember at one time these were the feelings you had.

Emma Keoghoe & Alice Olivia Larraine Brock (14)
Passmores Academy, Harlow

THE NANDO'S POEM!

When I go to Nando's I eat like a hippopotomus
And my refills are bottomless

When I get hot and spicy
I get all feisty

Your daughter is a liar
My mixtape is on fire

Yeah, yeah!

Chicken and rice
A glass of water would be nice

Piri-piri spicy and hot
I like the lot

You know the chicken
It's finger-lickin'.

Ellie Morgan (15)
Passmores Academy, Harlow

EVIL

When I close my eyes at night
The war I just begin to fight
Visions of light disappear
And nightmares reappear
Shrivelling with fear
That my screams no one will hear
The devil is right here!

I opened my eyes at morning
I was so surprised to see
That it was all a dream
The devil is right here!
No it's not
It's all gone
Goodbye mysterious daydream.

Jasmine Burt (14)
Passmores Academy, Harlow

HARD TIMES

It's hard going in care
And when people stare,
The hard times don't fly by
They make all people cry,
You think they could stop
By grabbing the gun and taking a shot.

You sit in a room with the lights down
Looking around with your face in a frown,
You see your mum crying her eyes out
Then know where you are then begin to pout,
The hard times you think
It's all never done,
I'm in heaven now
The hard times they have all gone!

Emily Evans (14)
Passmores Academy, Harlow

MY POEM ABOUT SCHOOL

School sucks, school's boring
Teachers begin yapping, meanwhile everyone's snoring
Covering stuff we already know
When you say it's too easy, they say, 'So?'
They moan at you for talking to your friends
When they speak the lecture never ends

I'm going to keep this simple
What's the point of school?
We already know it all
I'm going to keep this short
Get on your feet teachers
And do something fun . . .
For once!

Bradley Hayden Arnold (14)
Passmores Academy, Harlow

MUSIC

Music changed my life, it's the best
Thing in my world, I don't have
A favourite genre, but I like certain songs

Music is important to me, it brings out
My personality, when I listen
To it the world stops

Music is like a person, it can
Be sad or happy, but I will
Never hate it

The only message I'm trying to
Say, is that music can
Change your life.

Robyn Iona Fell (14)
Passmores Academy, Harlow

REMEMBRANCE

Remember, remember
Those who risked their lives
They gave their everything
So we could have anything

Remember, remember
To wear your poppy
Pay your respects
And don't be sloppy

Remember, remember
17 million dead
And 20 million wounded for so many
Hopes and dreams were ruined.

Kimberley Airlie (14)
Passmores Academy, Harlow

PRIDE

Every nation, north, east, south and west
Coming together to see who's the best
Their will to survive is put to the test
Playing every contest like it's life or death

After eighty minutes all muscles utilised
All people left brutalised
Everyone cheering for man of the match
Every try, kick and catch

Sportsmanship is key
So everyone takes a knee
While the national anthems are played in symphony
Every player feels courage, strength and empathy.

George Bright (14) & Lewis
Passmores Academy, Harlow

THE MONSTER

The monster is within everyone
It hides but is not hidden
When it's found within someone
It gets removed and becomes forbidden
In the good man is evil
And in the evil man is good
All evil are the devil
And all good are Robin Hood
The secrets of the monster are mysterious
But can be so very clear
The monster is very curious
To find these secrets can take all year.

Robert Judd (15)
Passmores Academy, Harlow

TEENAGE LIFE

Teenage life is like the weather
Sometimes sunny and sometimes dull
Some people have colourful souls
And some have dark souls
At times life gets you down
Sometimes acts like a clown
In life love can be magic
At times it can be tragic
Most times I'm chilling, playing video games
The adrenaline is turning me to flames
At times like this, education is important
But messing around is unimportant.

Hallie Green (14) & Marilia Sofia Pais De Abreu Costa (15)
Passmores Academy, Harlow

A YOUNG GIRL

A young girl only ten years old
Already her body is being sold
She doesn't want to live this life
So she puts up a fight
Asking people to let her go
She wonders why they won't leave her alone?
Put into care at the age of two
She doesn't know what to do
She sits every night crying
People always say she's lying
Her life is full of hate
All she wants is a mate.

Kayleigh Woods (14)
Passmores Academy, Harlow

THE INNER SELF DARKNESS

As I looked in the mirror
All I could see was the cold-hearted monster in the inner self
All the bad was catching up to me
All I could see was his black heart
It was as black as a dark night
You couldn't see his face
It's covered with a dark fog
It was building up, the more bad he does
The bigger the dark fog gets
Every cold and dark night
I just keep on fighting, fighting
Just to not let the darkness inside me come out.

Shannon Pickering (14)
Passmores Academy, Harlow

BULLIES

Every lunchtime you pick on me
Every lunchtime you push me
Punch me, take the mickey out of me
Four years of the same pain and embarrassment
With no one to turn to
I feel smaller and smaller and smaller each time
It's got to the stage where I'm harming myself
Every time I get home I wear a false smile upon my face
So my parents don't worry about me
Your voice rings through my head and you shout at me
You've ruined me!

Bailey Spencer Nicklen (14)
Passmores Academy, Harlow

SCHOOL

School can be boring
School can be interesting
Some lessons fly by but others take time
Every day I wake up early
And make my hair curly
Just to sit here being bored
Between these four walls
Waiting for the bell to ring
When it does we all cheer and sing
Once they're all over we scream, cry
Screaming and waving the day goodbye.

Rebecca Porter (14)
Passmores Academy, Harlow

THE HAND IN NEED

He handed her a helping hand
When she was down
As the girl cried more,
It started to look like a well
As tears ran down her face
The girl become more and more sad
The boy stepped forward to give her a helping hand
The girl looked up and began to smile
That's the help of the helping hand.

Macy Hannaford (14)
Passmores Academy, Harlow

WHY I HATE POEMS

Poems are stupid and dull
Don't get me wrong, that's just my opinion
So next time someone asks me to read a poem
I will stand up to the status quo and say no

And before you ask I don't have a choice
I didn't want to write a poem
I didn't want to use my voice.

Hollie Dawson (14)
Passmores Academy, Harlow

POEMS

Poems bore me, I don't like them
I think they're pointless
You think they're amazing
Why do some rhyme and others don't?
Why are some long and others short?
Poems are essays, just made to confuse me
Similes and metaphors trying to amuse me.

Kaylee Samuels (15)
Passmores Academy, Harlow

UNTITLED

People say I'm intelligent
But they're just irrelevant
Looking for the right path
Just after a laugh
Waiting for the good times
Whilst eating clementines.

Susie Green (14)
Passmores Academy, Harlow

BO 3

I've already played it for seven hours
It's like I've got super human powers
I played it for a long time
Then I made a long rhyme
Black Ops 3 is a good game
But people at it are really lame.

Tom Brown (14)
Passmores Academy, Harlow

THE MONSTER WITHIN

A secret everyone keeps
That makes everyone weep
It's there day and night
To give you a fright
They are always wrong
But they think they're right.

Rebecca Richardson (15)
Passmores Academy, Harlow

THE THING INSIDE

There is something inside of me
Just wait and see
And when you meet him you'll beg and plead
For it to be over, like a terrible dream.

Drew Cooper (14)
Passmores Academy, Harlow

GOOD AND BAD

Everyone is good
And
Everyone is bad
Some people show more than others

But
In every good
There is a
Bad
And
In every bad
There is a
Good

Some people's minds
Trigger
And
The bad side is set off
Punching, kicking and violence.

But
In every good
There is a
Bad
And
In every bad
There is a
Good

While others control the
Bad
Letting them release the
Good
They show kindness, love and happiness
I wish
That all people could.

Jaz Harvey (14)
Passmores Academy, Harlow

RUGBY

The Rugby World Cup is finally here
Everyone celebrating with a pint of beer
No one can wait for all of the plays
All of the players smothered in praise.

Sam Marston
Passmores Academy, Harlow

UNTITLED

Some may say a poem does not have to rhyme
All the time but when they do it's something brilliant
Like a Christmas morning when it starts snowing
Or a moment of relief when you find your parents
In the shop after being lost
But as you can already see
No matter how small you are
You can become bigger.

Owen Sharpe (14)
Passmores Academy, Harlow

CONFIDENT

We are loud, we laugh
We sing and dance
People judge us for how we look
And how we act
We want to ignore their stares
But sometimes we put on an act
Sometimes our confidence breaks
We don't let it show

We don't care about what we wear
We just want to have fun
People assume we just want to be young
We want to ignore the remarks
But we look at ourselves and think we are not perfect
Sometimes our confidence breaks
We won't let it show

We are kids, we don't understand
We just think everything's okay
People don't tell us the truth
We are too young and carefree
We want to be responsible but we can't be trustworthy
But people judge us by our reputation
Sometimes our confidence breaks
We should let it show
We are all the same
We are all confident even if you don't let it show.

Harrlet Wakefield (11)
St Albans Girls' School, St Albans

FINE LIES

Her life fails her,
It's a shattered mirror,
She blames herself,
She's a burden to her soul.

It's gone way beyond her limitations,
She doesn't want to harm,
She doesn't want to commit.

Nobody has the time to realise,
She doesn't blame them,
Everybody is just so caught up in their own lives.

She's fine to see that you don't know,
She's fine being alone,
Despite having you.

She's being patient for the angel of death,
She's ready for the hardship after death.

Silence revolves around her nights,
No sleep,
Just a girl wide awake,
Whose silent tears flow down her face,
She shows no emotion,
No intention of tears,
Yet she's so lost into the silent dark.

Is anybody going to save her?
Bring her back to once upon a time?
Be there for her anytime she needs you?
Can you tell there's something wrong without asking her?
Or
Are you going to believe her 'I'm fine' lies?
Her fine fake laughter?
Her fine fun days?
Are you happy to let her die without knowing she died unhappy?

Mashiath Choudhury (15)
St Albans Girls' School, St Albans

THE LONELY TREE

I am a tree and not as happy as can be
How it happened I'm really not sure
But Christmas came and knocked on my door
The next thing I know before I could speak
They were covering me in twinkly things
Flash, flash, it's all I could see
You invaded my space and were hurting me
You took me away from my forest of friends
And then I was lonely and saw the end
You chopped off my branches and cut off my leaves
I'd been growing them for ages, can't you see?
I could smell the fire and burning wood
Would I become fire, I'm not sure I should
If my mum was here I would have let her know
And you would have been kicked out and covered in snow
You decorated me like a doll, stuck me in a hole
And now what's next for me – *coal?*
But I had a plan, a really good plan
On Christmas Day when they were eating their ham
I would topple over, smash a window
And then I would be kicked out and covered in snow
They would never be able to find me, never, ever, ever
And then I would grow tall again and that would be better
I would move far, far away back to my forest of friends
And then hopefully that would be the end
Oh yes, by the way I am now living the life with my forest of friends
And now no longer can I see the end.

Emma Durkin (11)
St Albans Girls' School, St Albans

WHAT A DAY!

There once was a silent avenue
Where raindrops fell from the trees
Not a chirp, not a breath, not a whisper
Just an autumn morning swift breeze

The time was quarter past seven
So no blue sky for them yet
Most people were still tucked in warm
While the cars were outside soaking wet

Some people remember it's work day
So they stomp their feet on the floor
Which alerts every bird, everybody
As you hear the slam of the door

The postman's up doing his duty
Which means all the dogs have a bark
Eventually their owners crawl out of bed
And stop the loud hounds in the dark

Now some more people have woken
Awake but still half asleep
Making toast for the entire household
Watching the frosty wind leap

Now almost everyone is up and dressed
All the kids watching TV
While the babies cry their eyes out
The dads are watching rugby

Mums scurry round hunting for things
Her purse, her shoes, her handbag
All the three brothers play video games
Whining loudly because of a lag

The time is almost ten thirty
The girls have to go to ballet
Dragging the dads and the brothers
To watch them in their brand new play

Children are scoffing packed lunches
Getting set for a long ride
Their nan's smothering them in some suncream

Even though all day they're inside

Mums have to drive home from work now
To take the dog on a long walk
But she chats to her friend the whole time
While the dog just sits through their talk

The teenagers late from school again
Having a secret trip to town
Parents yell as they waste money
On a very expensive silk gown

The family get together for dinner
Spaghetti mixed with Mum's hair
While the children eat politely
Babies make mess everywhere

They're choosing a Saturday night film
Under blankets at half past nine
The toddlers scream while the teens laugh
As appearing on screen is Frankenstein

The children are tucked up in bed now
The teenagers texting all night
The parents have a minute of relaxing
Before hearing the baby needs light

Now the house is all silent
Not much crying compared to the day
The parents are absolutely exhausted
In their minds they think, *What a day!*

Louise Deans (11)
St Albans Girls' School, St Albans

SORRY MY DEAR PAM

It's dark, it's cold
I think I know where I am
Away from the life I left behind
I am sorry my dear Pam

Hidden behind my only hope of life and love
Scared and alone I beckon for you

The stars are shining like your eyes
But the shine disappears and I awaken to horror

It's starting again, the blood will be shed
Every man for himself, no aid will be given
Ready and waiting, I hide with fear
The roller coaster will start again

Ready, set, charge

I will never forget the screams and cries
Of all the men left behind

Then I fall, stumbling to the ground
One last bang is the final sound

It's dark, it's cold
I think I know where I am
Away from the life I left behind
I am sorry my dear Pam.

Emily Frangiskou-Hemming (14)
St Albans Girls' School, St Albans

THE POETRY TRIALS - HERTFORDSHIRE & ESSEX

LIFE VS CANCER

Dedicated to fighters out there; there is a can in cancer, because we CAN beat It.

They wake up in pain and agony,
Watching each second as it goes.
The monster growing inside of them,
Yet this is not the life that they chose.

It kills them day by day,
But the warriors still fight.
They live life, doing whatever they can,
To make it to bed tonight.

Walking down the wards,
And on constant medication.
It makes them feel so wretched,
So full of frustration!

But I want to be the one,
Who will find the cure some day.
This twisted disease will vanish,
And everyone will be okay.

I know we will all go,
But life is too precious to lose.
So hold on to it while you can,
Because it's not something you can reuse . . .

Irsa Khan (14)
St Albans Girls' School, St Albans

AUTUMN IS THE BEST SEASON!

A utumn is a beautiful season
U mbrellas are always needed
T omorrow the leaves will fall whilst others change colour
U nravelling whilst falling like a feather
M oving, rustling
N obody knows what colours the leaves will turn, maybe from red to orange or yellow to brown

I t is always lovely for children
S o get on your wellies!

T his is the only time to kick leaves
H er name is Autumn
E very year she puts on her wellies and goes to have fun

B ecause the leaves are beautiful
E very year it gets better and better
S oon it is over
T omorrow more fun will begin

S easons are the best time of the year
E verything goes silent
A utumn, can you hear children kicking leaves?
S oon the children will bury themselves
O n the leaves that have just fallen
N obody wants autumn to end.

Rachel Staples (11)
St Albans Girls' School, St Albans

CHRISTMAS

C hristmas is the best time of the year
H earing everyone laugh and cheer
R inging your family on the phone
I n the snow they are not alone
S nowing, hailing, raining lots
T he time is coming where it is not hot
M y family, friends, opening presents
A s the sun sets the snow looks like a desert
S tockings filled on Christmas Eve

I t is almost time to leave
S anta Claus you hear him go

T ime went fast and the snow
H ad some sunburn and melted below
E veryone wakes up on Christmas morning

B et everyone is yawning
E verybody is happy and smiling
S anta won't be back for a while
T hat's why Christmas is the best!

Chloe May Southall (11)
St Albans Girls' School, St Albans

WINTER

A kaleidoscope of colours forms in front of my excited eyes
As the exploding fireworks zoom into the sky
Whilst impressing the people with their marvellous colours
The icy cold wind gently touches my red rosy cheeks
As the emerald grass sways in the beautiful winter breeze
Swiftly falling down like a feather
The gold and red leaves make their way down to the orangey ground
And bury themselves as if they were ancient treasures
The bare trees wave to the people below
Whilst the icy cold lake reflects the memories above
Astonishing flames rise before me
With people cheering along
The poppies quietly stand around
Eagerly watching the fire grow
Suddenly the flakes fall onto the delicate ground
Making everything as white as a pearl
Snowmen appear everywhere
Being treated and cared with cute little hats and scarves
Glistening under the frozen white trees
The icicles hang upside down
Christmas lights are *everywhere*
With people waiting for gifts and presents
And children waiting for Santa Claus to be found.

Samiha Thakur (12)
St Albans Girls' School, St Albans

SUMMER

 S ummer is the perfect time of the year, the hot blazing sun and the thin air
 U nder the sun getting the perfect tan before autumn
M elting ice cream dripping onto my hand
M aroon coloured leaves have disappeared
 E venings are shorter but the day is longer! Woo hoo!
 R ed, purple, orange: lots of colours that remind me of summer.

Ranya Ramdani (11)
St Albans Girls' School, St Albans

AUTUMN TO WINTER!

Autumn turns orange and red
Winter creeps in and turns into white
In autumn you snuggle in bed
In winter you smile at the mystical sight

The trees change colour
From green to red
The conkers fall down onto your head
In the piles of leaves
In the sound of squirrels scratching on trees
Forms the cheerful season
Autumn!

The sun starts to sleep
The snowflakes drift
In the cold frozen breeze
In the time when you freeze
Forms the magical season
Winter!

After this happens you will not forget
The memories you've created
When autumn turns into winter!

Marika Stefani (11)
St Albans Girls' School, St Albans

HOLIDAYS

H appy times
O f
L oving and enjoying
I ce skating and sunbathing
D aily for each
A mazing day of your time off. Eating
Y ummy
S weets on your holiday!

Elena Cobb (11)
St Albans Girls' School, St Albans

CHOCOLATE IS YUM

Chocolate, chocolate, yum, yum, yum!
I can't wait till it goes in my tum
It's even better than gum
It melts in my mouth in the south
Because it's so hot, hot, hot
My brother and sister like it a lot
We share it at night in the dimmest light
Everyone can't wait to bite, bite, bite
As soon as I bite it my mouth waters
My mum slices it in quarters
We have it at Christmas, summer and autumn
Especially Easter, Easter, Easter
Chocolate is my life
I cut it with a knife
Tomorrow I have it,
The next day I will have a bit
My gran will have it when she knits, knits, knits
If I didn't have chocolate I don't know what I'd do
When my family have it we all shout, 'Whoo hoo!'
So I think we all know that chocolate is even better than gum
Because it's so yum, yum, yum!

Emily Branston (11)
St Albans Girls' School, St Albans

FRIENDS

F riends last forever
R easons people should have friends are: comfort, for help, kindness and they stand by your side
I n everyone's heart there's a place for a friend you just have to find one
E ven if you're being bullied a friend will stand by your side
N ever will a friend hurt you, they will help you if you are hurt
D eath will not be the end of friendship only if you choose.

Kayleigh Hardwick (11)
St Albans Girls' School, St Albans

MY BED

When I wake up in the morning
To see the shining sun
I'm trapped
I can't get out
I'm in my bed

When I come home from school
All I really want is my bed
A heavenly feeling drawing me in
It's pulling me closer
I'm in my bed

When it comes to dinner
I can't help myself
A puff of cloud tempting me in
I'm in bed

Finally when it's time for bed
I'm so happy
I could fly
'Cause guess what?
I'm in bed.

Mahjabeen Choudhury (11)
St Albans Girls' School, St Albans

WOLF

W onderful creatures
 O ver they leap and through the snow
  L ong sharp teeth cut through their prey
   F rom the hands of God these creatures were made.

Amelie Wood (12)
St Albans Girls' School, St Albans

THE PERFECT CHRISTMAS MORNING

The moment your eyes peep open, when you hear the roaring silence and get an exciting tingle run through your whole body.
The only time you want to leap out of your bed to celebrate the holiday of Christmas
You check the end of your bed and see your stocking full to the brim, stuffed with treats.
You tiptoe out of your room to wake up your sisters to see who has the most presents
Then you sneak into your parents' room and ask if you can open your presents
Then you get that disappointing feeling when your parents say, five more minutes.
So you decide to peep out of your window and see the glistening snow falling from the sky.
That's what makes a perfect Christmas!

Amber Durrant (11)
St Albans Girls' School, St Albans

ROLLER COASTER

R olling down the track
O ver the ground and under tunnels
L oudly everyone screams!
L oops are ahead of us. Uh oh!
E veryone is scared
R olling wheels get faster and faster

C olliding along the track
O h no! We are at the top
A rgh!
S uddenly it's going faster than ever
T hen hands go up in the air
E veryone screams again
R apidly, the roller coaster has ended its journey.

Abby Farnsworth (11)
St Albans Girls' School, St Albans

WINTER

Winter is finally here
When Christmas comes all the adults will be drinking beer
Snow will come
Children will finally be having fun
With sledges and snowball fights
They will do it with all of their might
And adults will join in with all of their rights
To act like a child once again
From all the hard work and
The fun they just earned
But they all cry in such pain
As love is back here in time
As we sit as a family saying
All of our rhymes
Christmas plays start as they all say their lines
As winter is finally here!

Shakhreen Thoyeba Miah (11)
St Albans Girls' School, St Albans

THE BOOK THAT TRANSPORTS

Animated to the world I had entered,
neglectful of the world I had left behind.
Idle to cacophony around me,
floating on an idyllic thread that carries and never tires.

Unconscious of the congregations and sounds.
Hesitant passengers,
made calm by our earth falling behind them,
our transport that embezzles negative sentiment.

The words that entwine and comfort me,
used as a weapon in my past, drove me from this world.
This world that is now my home, smaller than an ingot,
concealed in a prison that only the literate can break,
a book . . .

Sophia Laycock (13)
St Albans Girls' School, St Albans

ONE DAY

What if our world was at peace for one day?
Talking, listening, debating
Replacing fighting, bombing and killing
It's fine for me but look through her eyes
See what she can see
Frightened families fleeing their homes
Leaving everything they have ever known
Houses like skeletons, the flesh is gone
Communities torn apart by war and poverty
Women mistreated and not given a voice
Love, equality, peace
Over injustice, prejudice and terrorism
No one should have to live in fear
If our world was at peace for one day
Peace could be reality not just a dream.

Kirsty Reed (12)
St Albans Girls' School, St Albans

WHY?

Why did you leave?
Did you actually care?
About all the memories that we shared

Remember the times we used to talk
2am on your red tiled rooftop
Words filled with lustful eyes and passionate love
Our drunk words were our sober thoughts
They all said we didn't know what love is
I say we were just not right for this
It was just a matter of time
For our arguments to cross the line
Why did you leave?
You said forever despite pain
But you still left me crying in the pouring rain.

Jemima Biodun-Bello (13)
St Albans Girls' School, St Albans

THE POETRY TRIALS - HERTFORDSHIRE & ESSEX

TREES

In the winter, the trees are bare,
With snow covering the branches,
And squirrels hiding in their secret lair.
In the spring, the trees have flowers, with bright
Green leaves, they grow as tall as towers.
In the summer, the fruits start appearing, with the
Sun shining down on them, and below the trees, the
People start cheering. In the autumn,
The leaves turn brown, with
Orange and red colours,
And the
Leaves
Start
Falling
Down,
Ready
For
Winter
Again.

Millie Walker (11)
St Albans Girls' School, St Albans

FAMINE – AN GORTA MÓR

Love, separated
Love, tears as the prison ships came
Love, you steal
Love, lost
Love.

Hunger, starving
Hunger, searing pain
Hunger, no food in sight
Hunger, everywhere
Hunger.

Desperation, crying
Desperation, death
Desperation, screams
Desperation, always
Desperation.

Famine, black crop
Famine, no food
Famine, no money
Famine, rotten
Famine.

Smell, sweet
Smell, rotten
Smell, decay
Smell, unthinkable
Smell.

The unforgettable sight of the famine ruined all,
The way it affected life, history and especially Ireland wasn't fair.
Now Ireland is known for bad reasons; the way they suffered
Unprepared for what happened
Pray for all of those who experienced this
And pray it won't happen again.

Danielle Martin
St Benedict's Catholic College, Colchester

BLIGHTED LIFE

I was sown on a late spring evening
Hugged by the soil that was stinking
I stared up into the sky
But the stars were too high
As the darkness sucked me in
I knew life would be dim

It's June now but it's grim
My plant has been trimmed
I felt ill and sad
But the rash was just too bad
My rash was black
But my neighbour had been pulled out

I felt a squeeze on my leaves
And I looked towards the trees
The farmer pulled me out
But dropped me to the ground
He opened his mouth
And gasped out loud

Then the farmer committed a sin
He threw me in the bin
The blight had bitten
And among the rubbish I was hidden.

Bandi Cserep (12)
St Benedict's Catholic College, Colchester

AN GORTA MÓR

In the summer of 1845, a terrible fate befell
The poor, impoverished people of the Emerald Isle
A vile disease proliferated through the potato crop
Which led the population to a massive drop
The vital potatoes, covered in blight
The poverty-stricken people left to die
Children suffered, men tried hard
To ensure that their families did not starve
The potatoes were what they were fed
So losing their food source was their main dread
The famine left thousands of victims dead
And most who survived soon turned and fled
They headed for the Canadian coast
In what became known as coffin boats
The perilous journey across the sea
Was not the success they hoped it would be
Hundreds died of typhus and dysentery
And the welcome for survivors was at best frosty!
The effects of this disaster can still be seen
The population's not recovered to what it had then been.

Maddie Barrell (11)
St Benedict's Catholic College, Colchester

DINNER TIME

Dustbins optimistic, their voluminous depressions fly open
Perfunctory functions slide down the fridge impediment
Hindering it more oppressively
Frequently, frequently on, still on!
Like grinding cogs of explosive, extensive wide crushers
Gushing liquids flood down the river conduit
Echoes fly out, like bubbling monsters
Computers rise, sluggishly its motorised executions shuffle to the glittering drencher
Returning, reversing to its mission.

Amaia Lilia Jane D'Souza (12)
St Benedict's Catholic College, Colchester

AN GORTA MÓR

My street, full of Irish blood, cried with fear and agony
The Irish nation brought down to dust
The Irish nation evaporated with each dead potato
The Irish nation had finally met the airborne disease, the blight

The blight ripped through each wave of innocent pedestrian families
The blight forced the innocent to travel in their own coffin
To the Promised Land, America

America, full of new chances and possibilities
Was the light of hope for the Irish
New York, Chicago or even Mississippi
Gave the Irish a chance to start over

Across the Atlantic, the UK stood strong
In giving the Catholic infested Irish a cruel Protestant beat down
The Irish overcame their problems and stood strong together
And lived in harmony with the English till this day
The Irish have lost their former glory
But regained it with confidence that has lived long till this day.

Zylo Green
St Benedict's Catholic College, Colchester

AN GORTA MÓR

A gony clung to my broken soul
N othing left; just a monstrous hole

G one was Cabhan; departed was my darling, Glannah
O nly I was left, waiting for death's clutch
R ot had desensitised me, life wasn't worth much
T hirsty for freedom; hunger turned me to sorrow
A ll dreams turn towards Chicago

M any made the voyage, ignoring dangers
O n the way in 1947, I died alone among expiring strangers
R emember me and the great hurt!

Inge-Maria Christine Botha (12)
St Benedict's Catholic College, Colchester

THE CURSE OF FREEMANTLE BAY

The people of Ireland tremble in fear
At the mention of this cursed place

Where good honest men were sent
For the crime of feeding their families
For the crime of making sure
Their children saw the morning

The prison ship's port
Throwing men into a situation worse than death
A life without love
A life of living in a barren, merciless wasteland
And a life not knowing if your loved ones survived the dreaded famine

The people of Ireland tremble in fear
At the mention of this cursed place
A place devoid of culture, belief and hope
Excommunicated from the curse of Freemantle Bay.

Shannon Payne
St Benedict's Catholic College, Colchester

YOU, ME AND THE FAMINE

As the moon rises in the Irish night
The beloved potato is infected with blight
Then as the sun rises over the rooftops
Farmers come out to harvest their crops

As they pull the crop from the earth
They stagger back onto the turf
Their food is gone, all hope is lost
They might as well throw it onto the compost

Then occurs theft, starvation, emigration
People decide to leave their glorious nation
But not me, oh no, I stay
I ask God, 'Why is this happening? Why must we pay?'

Tom Brown
St Benedict's Catholic College, Colchester

THE GREAT FAMINE

The Great Famine of Ireland
Started with a blight in their farmland
People were starved
Left the country empty and sad

Their crops were destroyed
Irish people were annoyed
People have cried
And their animals left to die

They travelled to a far away place
To find a good and abundant space
How lucky for some may be
To have found a place that is so wealthy
Oh how pitiful were they
They were scattered like hay
In the end anyway
They lived so happy and gay.

Natasha Gail Escabarte
St Benedict's Catholic College, Colchester

THE BLACK HARVEST

B roken hearts and broken families
L onging for food, longing for love
A nxious and scared we take drastic measures
C alling for help but no one listens
K eeping hope deep in our hearts

H ungry and starving
A nyone and everyone
R uns from this curse
V ery few survive
E mpty and lost, Ireland cries for her children
S puds disappear when we need them most
T his is the Black Harvest!

Chenile Sulley
St Benedict's Catholic College, Colchester

THE GREAT FAMINE

I woke up in the morning to the smell of mould and rot
I looked out the window and saw my potato crop

Potatoes are the staple of Ireland
We need them to survive

While the British crawl and roll in gold
We try to find food to strive

As people fail to conquer death
I get nearer to my last breath

The man is there and he has corn
I take it, I am captured, sentenced and to be sent away at dawn

In the warship I smell death
I look around, the gun is there, *bang*, I meet my end

I hope my wife can still live on
Surviving off the food I have won.

Olivia Farry
St Benedict's Catholic College, Colchester

THE SUN

The sun, the sun, it shines down on us so we can have fun
The sun, the sun, we see it one day, every day
It shines so bright because it knows it's a bit right
Because it goes down without a fight
Orange, red and a little bit yellow
It flies in the sky just like a large pillow
As we eat, drink we're always just there
With the sun giving us a big stare
It's time for dinner
And the sun is getting thinner
It's time for bed
And the sun sinks like a small bit of lead.

Kyeron David Holmes (11)
Tabor Academy, Braintree

THIS IS WAR

Blood, death and noises
Louder than your own thoughts.
This is war.
Cold, dark. lonely nights,
No sounds, just silence.
This is war.
Waiting for the signal
To attack. Scared, alone, worried.
This is war.
Distant memories flash by.
Every moment of the day.
This is war.
Friends, here today,
Dead tomorrow.
This is war.
Family worries grow
Day by day. Not knowing.
This is war.
Gunshots boom! Flying past
My ears. A hit is certain death.
This is war.

My turn. I run. Heart beats louder than ever before,
Fear surrounds me. Death coming closer to me.
I am hit. I stop. I fall. I lay in sludge.
I see ... I see my family, my loved ones ...
Take me. Take me home God. Take me home.
This is war.

Freddy Braniff (11)
Tabor Academy, Braintree

A WINTER'S MORNING

I woke up early in the morning
Walked to my window and pulled at the blind
This is when my mum called out and gave me a warning
The light poured through the glass and what do I find?

Untouched snow, beautiful and white
I ran down the stairs as fast as lightning
Where I was told that I can't go out, and my fists clenched tight!
She said she was only joking and my face started brightening

I sprinted up the stairs and thew on my winter clothes
Then provided myself with my sledge
I open the door and in the wind flows
And wait for company on edge

My friends all arrive and we start to trudge
Then soon we enter the gate of the busy park
With snowballs in our hands people start to judge
And the sky becomes dark!

The snow rapidly fell from the sky
I started to run home as fast as I could
My day was ruined, I started to cry
I was embarrassed and pulled over my hood

My mum called me down
The kettle boiled with steam
Then I saw something brown
Then she came into the lounge
With a mug of hot chocolate and marshmallows and cream!

Katie Lesiak
Tabor Academy, Braintree

UNTITLED

As I twirl around the world
My fire onesie always stays tight
My heart heats me up so it's just right

If you hear explosions it means you're close to my heart
Every morning of every day I watch every step from every person
And my heart thumps louder as my smile gets bigger

See my wild hair, orange hair
It's pretty rare
Don't be worried we can share a warm friendship
But don't come too close, I burn so bright I can make you blind

The deodorant that I wear is called Smoky Ashes
Its smell is strong
And its lasting is long

As I twirl around the world
I glance upon everyone and say
I will always be the heat to your soul
And I will always be by your side
Even though I'm 149.6 million km away

I'm a very bright thing
I am the sun!

Brooke Moore
Tabor Academy, Braintree

STARS

I look up at the night sky and what do I see?
Lots of little stars shining down on me
Twinkling in the darkness like diamonds in the sky
I would love to reach up and touch them but they are just too high!
Some nights I dream of being a star way up in the sky
I'd get to meet the moon, even maybe learn to fly
But I know my family would miss me
So I'll let my dream fly by.

Ellie Stewart (11)
Tabor Academy, Braintree

BRIGHT LIGHT

I'm so hot, I'm so hot
Check me out, check me out
I'm hot, yo everyone, I'm made of gas like hydrogen and helium
I keep the Earth warm and help grow food,
I shine on the beach, set to the west, then comes the night
Then I rise from the east with that golden light
I'm so hot, so hot and bright, 28 million degrees
I make plants grow like trees and flowers
So powerful, I've got that solar power that makes the deserts dry, makes the oceans rise
Don't stare right at me; I will hurt your eyes
I am just about one million miles wide,
I'm so big you can fit a million Earths inside
I'm the centre of the solar system
Can't you see, got so much gravity? I'm 4.5 billion years old
In Spanish everybody calls me Sol
When I'm not around you'll be feeling cold
I give peace to every heart, I go to sleep when it's dark
I can't cope when it's raining
I'm so hot, so hot
How hot am I?
So hot, so hot!

Alisha Oddy
Tabor Academy, Braintree

THE LIGHT

I looked out of my bedroom window
And wished I could catch the sun when it falls to Earth
It is so bright, so full of light
I wish I could hold it in my hands
I wish I was God
If I was God I would spread the light
All over the world.

Freddie Wacey
Tabor Academy, Braintree

MY BEST FRIEND

Some people may think this is really strange
But my best friend's not a boy
He doesn't play Xbox
In fact, a ball's his favourite toy

He's not one for conversation
He's really rather quiet
But I'm sure he knows what I'm saying
When I speak to him each night

He climbs upon the sofa
And lays upon my lap
I'm not sure if he realises
That he's far too big for that!

He's crazy and he's smelly
And his bark, it pops your ears
But I wouldn't be without him
I'm so glad that he is here

I'm sure you will have guessed by now
That my best friend is my collie
And that I love him more than anything
Even when he is all muddy!

Charlie Archer (11)
Tabor Academy, Braintree

LIFE OUTSIDE

(Lipogram: A)

I live with trees, for they become my home
I sleep under the moon, for it is my life
I hunt with the universe, for it is my tool
I drink from the pond, for it is my soul
The mother is my forest, for this, I'm in infinite debt.

William Henry Pegrum (13)
Tabor Academy, Braintree

SPIDERS

Spiders are the living garden killers,
Crawling under and over obstacles.
Sometimes even lazing about,
Like a rested butterfly in the sun.
In its very own home between the plants,
Usually known as the dreaded web.

Looking like a suspect of nature,
To being a natural killer in the garden.
The spider is a scary dark creature,
Appearing as mini land octopus.
With its incredible eight legs,
Ready to attack anything in its way,
The spider lives as a danger to the living.

The spider quickly emerges from its web,
Trapping its prey rapidly,
Wrapping it round and round,
Until there is no movement in its prey.
In a matter of seconds the kill is over.

Jack Pinner
Tabor Academy, Braintree

BUTTERFLIES

Butterfly, butterfly
Black and red
Sitting on the flower's bed
Drinking nectar from tulips and roses
Making bright and beautiful poses
Then flying away to some other flowers
Charming us and insects with their colourful powers
Fluttering silently all day long
But only when the summer comes along
When it's winter you won't see a glimpse
Of a beautiful butterfly, a wonderful prince.

Rachel Huxter
Tabor Academy, Braintree

MY POEM

I sung to the bees to come and help
We rushed towards the sun at the break of dawn
I leaned on the edge of the world, the bees leading the sun into my grasp
I gently clasped the sun into my jar and tied the lid on

I said goodbye to the honeybees and went home
I slid my hand into the bright ball of light, it felt like jelly and smelt like roasted marshmallows
It would call home whenever near a light source

With it I could do anything
I reached high to the heavens above, all the flowers survived the winter
And everyone was happy
It was the best, I was like a fairy

But like they say all good things come to an end
I tipped the sun into my sink and like magic
It flew home, leaving only a shimmer in the water.

Demi Castell
Tabor Academy, Braintree

BMX

Up and down the jumps we go
Down the hill and round the burm
Through the rhythm section we flow
The speed makes our tyres burn.

If you make the 'A' final
Eight gates to choose from
You must make this your quickest cycle
Go down the track like a bomb

Finish top three to get a medal
It shows how much you should pedal.

Joseph Little
Tabor Academy, Braintree

SEASONS

Spring smudged with shades of green
Budding trees stand proud and tall
Colour smeared across never-ending meadows
Bluebells blanket the ever-changing land.

Crayoned in bold colours, comes the summer
Cooling rivers splash down the creek
Fields of sunflowers bursting with colour
Horizons plastered by scenes of cherry blossom

Then autumn arrives in a flurry of leaves
Trees water coloured, red, orange and yellow
Golden fields of corn decorate the landscape
Ripe apples drop from trees

Inked in black and white comes winter
Blasting draughts of icy snow into the land
Naked trees form a forest of skeletons
Leaving the county bare.

Mae Warner (12)
Tabor Academy, Braintree

FIREWORKS

F ire at the bottom of my eyes
I 'm normally used for a rave
R ays explode out of me
E veryone hears me make overpowered noises
W hen I am seen I get cries, I get peace
O ver the sunset there I go
R ising in blissfulness
K nown as a big bang
S ilently falling down to the floor.

Freddy Thorogood
Tabor Academy, Braintree

NEW LIFE

A new life brings a new smile
A new glimmer in that someone's eyes
A new mind that will order them to have disagreements once in a while
A new mouth which will tell their truths and lies

A different hand that will comfort others
A different personality to make their friends laugh
A different hair colour which is not like their mother's
A different idea that will be used on someone else's behalf

An unseen trick that they've up their sleeve
An unseen talent which must not be named
An unseen taste in fashion that makes others want to leave
An unseen anger that needs to be tamed

A completely new person that has come to Earth
A completely new person which is what diamonds are worth . . .

Elisha Elliston
Tabor Academy, Braintree

LIGHTNESS

L ight is a helpful guide that leads the way
I t shines so bright
G oodness surrounds me
H igher and higher I reach for the light
T hankfully I grab the sun
N ever fearing darkness
E vening, night or sleep
S o peaceful every day
S leeping well at night.

Daniella Noble
Tabor Academy, Braintree

SOMETIMES

I like it up here
I get to see my family every day
They told me they like me keeping them warm with my light
But sometimes I feel lonely
Sometimes I want to be with them
They said I wouldn't fit in
That I'm too kind and loving
That because I smell of freshly cut grass they'd make fun of me
And that because my voice is high-pitched and I move slow I'd be left behind
Maybe they're right
Maybe I should stay up here
Because then I won't be left behind
I'll just stay here then
All alone
But I like it up here!

Jessica Rose Stewart (11)
Tabor Academy, Braintree

SONNET INFINITY

Stars will always show you infinity
A true sonnet shows this in every line
But this sonnet is a strange one to see
Infinity is the only great light
True sonnets are only about loving
And in turn start an eternal friendship
It is like a knife with a deadly sting
Only a Cupid knife puts lips to lips
But this sonnet has a strange and sad twist
One that is always seen by mortal eyes
The snake of pure love has already hissed
And all heaven above looks to the sky
And so ends the story of my true love
She was the only one – my peaceful dove.

Dexter Love
Tabor Academy, Braintree

PUMPKIN

I was still, quiet
Until
Light by a candle brought me back to life
The dark, cold, evil
Witches, skeletons, ghosts
Galore!
They point, excited
I flicker again, blushing
On and on the monsters come
Some are old and some are young
Some scream at me
I love this time of year
I hide when my light blows out
Ashamed
I was still, quiet.

Isabelle Louis (11)
Tabor Academy, Braintree

UNTITLED

N ever have I seen such beautiful sights
O verhead in wonder with an abundance of lights
R adiantly dancing all around
T ogether in unison, not making a sound
H overing majestically throughout the sky
E legantly floating slowly
R ituals say it's perfect for love
N o one around except our friends above

L iving spirits that embrace the night
I n days of old some would recite
G listening off the lakes below
H elping nature to express its glow
T ime will pass and generations move on
S o too will the lights, continuing their song.

Josh Stone
Tabor Academy, Braintree

THE MAGIC BOX

Inspired By 'Magic Box' By Kit Wright

I will put in the box
The first tooth ever lost
All the starvation of the children
I will put in the box
Some water full of memories
Dreams that turn the sun black
I will put in the box
Harmony from a saxophone
And the first future ever planned
And passed by nature's stone
My box is carved with sugar, ice and fire
I shall save people's lives
And my box shall be loved forever.

Isobel Watson
Tabor Academy, Braintree

THE SUN

The sun is as bright as a knife piercing straight through the heart
The sun is as sharp as a needle going through paper
The sun is as hot as a barbecue getting lit
The sun is as bright as a light
The sun fades gently across the Earth.

Nathan Innes (11)
Tabor Academy, Braintree

THE POWER OF LIGHT

C alm and relaxing is what I am named for
A nd glow into the world above
N ever one the same
D esire is what I am made for
L ight me
E xtinguish me.

Daisy Eastman (11)
Tabor Academy, Braintree

BE YOUR ONLY LEADER

Rain does not make you cry, but crying makes it rain
Strain is not for strugglers, but strugglers choose to strain
The pain inside you can't be tamed until the trainer wants to tame
Pain is not your leader, you control the pain
So live your life to its full extent, even if your path is bent.

Lana Josephine Donovan (12)
The Chauncy School, Ware

MY DREAMS

(Lipogram – No C)

It is somewhere I go,
When I sleep at night,
Off to another world snug and tight.
All the things that I love will be waiting for me,
To enjoy and make use of them . . . for free.
But tonight I feel as if,
Something terrible is going to happen.
My nerves stiffening, my heart thumping,
I wait for a long time,
But I still don't sense anything.

Suddenly it happens,
A great big shadow falls on me,
I see a figure, a bit like a werewolf.
It is just a dot but as it walks forwards,
It seems like something out of this world.
I am too afraid to wait any longer,
So I start running endlessly . . .
I shut my eyes, still running,
To think of something.

But after a while, I start falling,
Then suddenly again, I wake up.
And return to my own lovely world,
Where my dream falls to an end!

Kavinaya Shree Sivakumar (12)
The Chauncy School, Ware

ADVENTURES

Mum says we're going to the shops
But that sounds boring
I want an adventure!
We get into the spaceship
And Mum starts the engine
And the countdown begins
3, 2, 1 ... We have lift-off!
Out into the space road we go
We come to a standstill
Mum says it's a traffic jam
But I see a ladder
Climbing to the shops
We're off to the shops
The boring 'oring shops
Suddenly we've stopped
Mum says, 'We're stuck in a traffic jam'
But it's not to me
It's a towering space star!
The space star clears and we're on the move again
We're off to the shops
The boring 'oring shops
The ship is in sight
Mum parks the spaceship so we get out
Mum gets the trolley and we zoom into the shop
First to the bakery!
Now to buy some bread, milk and vegetables too
All done!
So it's time to go back home
I'm so very tired from my adventure
It's an adventure when we go to the shops
So when we go to the shops again
It will be a tiring adventure again!
Let's go to the shops to see the towering space star again
But for now
My adventure is over with a big, big wow!

Amy Gent (11)
The Chauncy School, Ware

A LITTLE WHITE LIE

Somewhere I know
Is a place I will trance
Where I am ensconced in the warmth of the night
At the siren of dusk.

It is a place I know well,
Therein rings a bell
It signifies
The start of a little white lie.

All the things that I love turn on me,
My life is in agony.
The world puts its weight on my shoulders,
Causing my life to turn into smudging smoulders.

Something terrible is happening -
My nerves stiffen and my heart skips a beat,
My height decreases and my body transforms into a smaller being
My being turns into a speckle – one drop.

I penetrate a hellish world.
Apocalyptic.
No one is around
One drop.

Fire, burning me
Buildings, crushing me
Earth, pressurising me
One drop.

My being turns back to my previous self,
Therein rings a bell,
It signifies
The end of a little white lie – for me.

The world of dreaming is transitory
It will come back to haunt you when you least expect it.

Josh Thomas Davies (13)
The Chauncy School, Ware

CYBER BULLYING

This is a problem
Of epic proportions
That has swept across the world
Some have been afflicted
All have been affected
It's going so fast
We can't even tell
But I do know one thing
That it should be stopped
And we need to act now!

It's quite petty really
Bullying behind a screen
It's just cowardly and mean
But it is a matter
That must be stopped
Let the world unite
To be rid of these fiends
So are you with me
Or not?
Let's solve this crisis, why not?

This is the poem
Of a caring child
Who just
Wants this nightmare
To end
With his hands
On his heart and
His head bowed down
Pleading for these people
To just change.

Thomas Protherough (11)
The Chauncy School, Ware

ADORNED IN WHITE

I know he is watching me
In the morning and at night
He is always flying over us
Adorned in white

I remember when he left
We watched him fly to another land
He never came home
His children didn't understand

I miss our chats
When he used to tell me about his heroic days
He was always so modest
He used to reject my praise

When I see the sun
On a gorgeous summer day
I know it's him up there
He even cheers me up when he has nothing to say

We were expecting letters
Handwritten with kisses and the opposite to perfection
But what we did get was painful and upsetting
With printed text and with zero affection

I couldn't bear being apart from him
Even though we're still together
He was just another casualty to them
He dropped like a feather

It was hard not to cry
We all had to be brave
God's looking after him now
We salute him at his grave.

Roseanna Drake (12)
The Chauncy School, Ware

WE SALUTE THEM OVER THEIR GRAVES

Here we stand proud and not concerned
Never did we know what happened
Now we have just learned
How the war did happen . . .

So many lives taken
Never did we know
Never did we hear
How they fought in the snow

Christmas came around
We all feel so guilty
In danger at the time
Needing a shelter

Time is here, Christmas Day
Germans and the British will never say
Happy never to ever see that day
As they are all held at bay

Here we stand still proud and still guilty
Their days have gone but still remembered
11th of the 11th
We salute them over their graves.

John Drake (11)
The Chauncy School, Ware

WHEN I GROW UP

This world is so beautiful. And yet everyone seems so afraid to reach their arms out, spread their fingers, and touch it. Run their fingers through the trees and wash their hands in the ocean. Wash away all the dirt and all the pain from the day; let hurt sink to the seabed where one day you may meet it again at rock bottom.

The world seemed so beautiful. Its soul crystalline and creamy held together by a mantle of velveteen fabric. A fabric so fine that a single cut into its cross-stitched seams causes the lakes of our land to dissipate into a toxic waste. Toxic with the minds of people who walk across this delicate world with limbs too solid. Hearts too bitter to taste and bodies which fall through the cracks they tear, left behind as man wades through the hurt and the hysteria; and our addled candours will cripple, lost.

This world *was* so beautiful. A collate of servility and humility, kindness and sobriety. But we lost our way. Our destination became the devastation of tolerance and diligence: our aim an array of unachievable magnificence for long lasting affluence in a swollen city where prosperity means impossibility and poverty apathy. They said we were community yet we were segregated by similarity, hostility, and infected by the sickness that is obsession. So ricocheting off the walls of an infinite universe, our cries of hurt and bane, I may just tell myself, to scorch the reality, when I grow up I want to be a kid again.

Alana Romagnoli (15)
The Chauncy School, Ware

LIFETIME

So many years
So many great memories
So many tears
So many sad stories

We choose how to listen to our life
We choose which path to take
Our life is like the sound of a drum or fife
It's giving me a headache

We have to grow up sometime
We have to decide where to go
How to stop time
Nobody will know

Life, life, life
That's what people think about
Without a doubt
When will time go?
I cannot tell for I do not know

Love is what really matters
So share it
Before everything shatters
It's enough to last a lifetime.

Olivia Cotgrave (12)
The Chauncy School, Ware

THE DAY I CAME

The day I came
Like a ton of bricks
The moor disappeared
Like a never-ending roller coaster
I am strong
I am unbeatable
Like a mighty king

The day I came
Like an aeroplane just about to crash
Like the heavens had opened
I am a weapon of mass destruction
Like a machine gun ready for action

The day I came
Like a bomb with no gravity
I spread my wings
Like an eagle ready to strike
I am fast
I am furious
Like a revving engine speeding through space.

Evie Gaze (11)
The Chauncy School, Ware

THE POETRY TRIALS - HERTFORDSHIRE & ESSEX

WAITING TO LIVE, WAITING TO DIE

Waiting to live
It's risky
But I've got to take it
Running on the battlefield with no protection
Like the President after his election

Waiting to die
Lying with a wound
I've got nowhere to go but home
I will still get my awards for dedication and courage

My little boy
Can't wait to see his face when I get home
My wife, crying all day
My mum and dad, praying

November 11th
Me in a wheelchair
In front of the cenotaph
With my boy, by my side until the end.

Thomas Offord (13)
The Chauncy School, Ware

IT'S STILL A DREAM

Dreams
They're a funny thing
You can get bad ones
Maybe an alarm bell *ding, ding*

A loud roaring lion may appear
A tiger too
Or you might get a kiss
Or even an 'I love you'

You might have nightmares
But don't be scared
It will be alright
So you don't have to call your dad

In bed
I snuggle up to my teddy
I close my eyes
Now I'm ready to see what lies ahead.

Katie Davies (12)
The Chauncy School, Ware

UNKNOWN

In this journey
We walk into the unknown
The clock's hand
Drags us towards it
A day packed with surprises
Our plans do not matter
We seem to deny the fact -
Unknown is our journey
Afraid of the unknown
Created by our imagination
What have we created?
In the unknown we have to delve
To look for the right answers
We have to be aware
When we step into the unexplored
To be a willing learner
We have to be accepting.

Rebekka Carter Elliott (12)
The Chauncy School, Ware

FIFA 16

The brand new game made by EA
Has just been released
Lionel Messi on the case
With the EA symbol on his chest
In the game the graphics are new
The players can run and defend
Even when Cristiano Ronaldo is on the ball
The keepers are finally good after many years
So when we make a toast we say cheers!
The price ranges may still be here
But players are affordable and trading is back
Now making squads is a whole lot easier
And good squads are so easy to make
Scoring goals and saving goals still makes people rage
Good game, good graphics, good player prices
This year's FIFA is amazing, we thank you EA!

Keelan Peake (11)
The Chauncy School, Ware

DAISIE

I'm sorry. I didn't mean it
As we stood there in our private corner
I watched your eyes well with tears
And your cheeks start to flush
Your tear-stained top drooping over your shoulders
While you looked at me with those big brown eyes
You slowly got up
I feel even worse now as I watch you silently shed tears
That run down your face
I suddenly feel horrible
I didn't realise what I had done
You told me everything with yet no words
Now I understand how you feel
Let me make it up to you.

Isabel Ogunyemi (12)
The Chauncy School, Ware

SPRING

Such a beautiful season
Surrounded by beautiful colours
The blue sky
The yellow sun
And the pink blossom that covers the trees like icing

The fresh new beginning
Blooming flowers
And newborn animals
A creation of new life
The start of a new life cycle

The season of spring
A religious time for some
But the Easter Bunny
And chocolate eggs
Create scenes of excitement.

Emily Grace Weatherall (15)
The Chauncy School, Ware

HAPPILY EVER AFTER ...

There's usually never a happily-ever-after
It just became a thing for laughter

There's sometimes fireworks or birds
In one there's even a terrible curse

Those people! That person!
They are so fearsome

That's what they yell
With joy and sounding louder than a bell

There's usually never a happily-ever-after
It's just a big blaster

Fireworks and beautiful cars
Or even lying under the pretty stars.

Simranjit Sekhon (11)
Valentines High School, Ilford

WAR IS . . .

War is a land of sadness
Where bombs and grenades fall
The sky is grey and fearless
Full of Adolf Hitler's army

War is a place of bombs
When fire starts to enlarge
Grenades fall down too
Bringing buildings to rubble

War is a sky of invisibility
Where Hitler's army are hiding in the clouds
Hitler waits until darkness
To shower the bombs over everyone

War is a place of fire
Where flames enrage everywhere
The firefighters are struggling and in need of help
To put the ferocious fire away

War is a place of alarms
Where everyone is told to run to safety
Everyone must stay safe
To be protected from Hitler's anger at the British

War is a place of guns firing
Firing on biased sides
The gun shoots and *boom* they are dead
Less soldiers mean less chance of winning

War is a place of rationing
Where people don't get as much food as they should
They struggle to survive every year
Even when it's cold in the winter!

War is a place of rubble
Where buildings fall down everywhere
The *boom* can be heard miles away
Warning everyone Hitler is coming

War is life in the trenches
Where mud and slime ooze everywhere
Blood and corpses are scattered everywhere

Showing they must work harder

War is a place of sadness
Everyone hates it
Just like me
And everyone around the world

War is a place of sadness
Where bombs and grenades fall
The sky is grey and fearless
Full of Adolf Hitler's army . . .

Arunan Nadarajah (11)
Valentines High School, Ilford

FREEDOM

Staring outside of life I only knew
I witnessed a sight that never would've come to me
A bird of pure white circled my dark body
It was flying around my cage – something I couldn't experience
It sang sweetly over my humble groan
It had a smile that embarrassed my frown
A life I've never heard of made mine seem bad
Worthless, not a life at all . . .
What still confused me was what difference is there between me and him?
Like butter and jam, milk chocolate and white chocolate
Peanuts and cashews – what's the difference?

Freedom is all I seek
Freedom is all I need
Freedom is the only thing I don't have
I will fight for it – fight for my rights
Difference is used against not only me but everyone
It's a weakness that anyone can access for free
It needs to be changed – immediately
No one should suffer (be treated differently)
Also they are treated differently for the wrong reason
It must go – it will go if I have anything to do with it.

Zarmina Usman Khanzada (11)
Valentines High School, Ilford

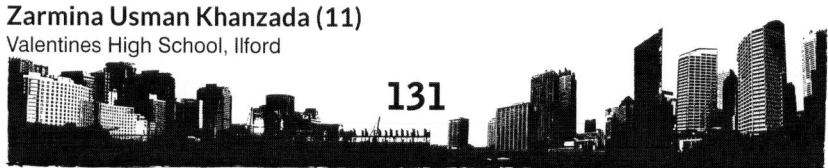

LOVE AND HELL

I sit on the floor
And take a deep sigh
I look at the faces
That pass by
I stare into their eyes
And wonder what life they have
The life I will never have
They must have kids
Who can't wait for their return
And busy wives cooking and looking after them
They are loved
And cared for by people
That is worth living for
And that's what counts

But my fate will not end happily
For I am an orphan
Not loved
Or cared for by anyone
Just regarded as unimportant
I have no home
No family to love
Or be loved
Just grief remains in the end

But I have hope
This gives me strength
And which is what everyone should have
No matter how lost
Or afraid anyone is
Hope is the strongest emotion
It defeats pain
And sorrow
With it
You can be the most important person in the world

Life is a gift
And is so fragile
Like breath on a mirror
It's there one second

And gone forever in the next
So treasure it
Every single second
Because now I won't feel sorry for myself
But look ahead and not waste a single second

Just me against the world.

Harris Bidiwala (12)
Valentines High School, Ilford

BODY OF THE SEA

Whoosh! An enormous hand of blue
Came through and then withdrew
Just then I knew
The sea went into
The Emerald Island
And far to the Highlands

As the sea went back
There was a crack
It all went black
The sun fell
It was hard to tell
If the night had come
My vision was glum

There were eyes
Big in size
Looking down
And around
Over the town

Whoosh! An enormous hand of blue
Came through and then withdrew
Just then I knew
The sea went into
The Emerald Island
And far to the Highlands.

Muhtasim Abrar
Valentines High School, Ilford

FOOTBALL

I was excited, to play with Manchester United
I thank my former mentor Mitch
Who led me onto the pitch
My heart was beating fast
I was finally on the pitch at last

Fans looked at my name as we started the game
I showed off my skills
To pay off my bills
Towards the goal I raced
Dribbling the ball at my pace
As sweat drizzled down my face
The crowds cheered
Until I was tackled
It was Bale
He looked at me as if I was a fail
He ran down the wing as fast as light
Not even using a bit of might
He took a shot with power
Zooming past the all-star defence
It was up to the hands of the keeper
But nothing could stop the power from Bale
Manchester United were on their knees
Nothing more could make them pleased

I had to score to liven up the game
Maybe then I will have my fame
I dribbled past the opponent like never before
I took a shot with a roar
And that is when I finally scored
This was a thing to remember
That I scored on the 5th of November.

Rameez Taha Haider (11)
Valentines High School, Ilford

NO SUMMER LASTS FOREVER

One winter night
Is a night of winter white
A soft wind blows
A new layer of snow
The beautiful sky is black while the dirty ground is white
Places are shimmering on the wintry night.

Not even a sound to be heard
Just the beautiful chirping of the bird
Slipping and sliding on the sea
The wind creeps up behind me
Smooth and clean and frosty white

I guess I'll hang around
Because I'm frozen to the ground
Watch the frozen snow
When it falls you see every bit glow
A bright blue sky
By a gust of wind was pushed aside

I made some PJs and a pillow for its head
Then last night it ran away but first it wet my bed
At night don't make a peep
In the morning the snow will be deep
Everyone hates frozen toes

While others cry about a runny nose
Temperatures so low
Though howling winds still blow
Slow beats of winter rain
Poor foolish little drops down, dripping all in vain
No summer lasts forever, no winter skips its turn.

Aysha Hussain (11)
Valentines High School, Ilford

PHANTOMS OF THE NIGHT

Don't see them in the light
But when you go to bed
Just to give you the fright
Wander around these phantom spirits
In your house and your garden
They never will make a sound
I ask myself, 'Is it my imagination?
Or really in fact
They're one of God's wondrous creations?'

I cannot sleep knowing they dance in my house
I shiver with fear
Whilst they give one good browse
I sit up
The moonlight hits me
I realise there is nothing to be scared of really
Or maybe . . . ?

I jump out with great massive fear
'What was that?'
I ask myself almost making a tear
That ticklish chill comes back again
The misty-looking figure comes and whispers
'Let's go home'

My skin turns pale
I can't feel the floor
I follow the figure
I am no human no more.

Ishrak Sarar Hossain
Valentines High School, Ilford

CURIOUS CLOUDS

Every day the sun and moon appear
But the clouds disappear
The clouds try to appear
But soon the moon and the sun prevent them
The clouds get smaller
While the sun and the moon get bigger

And again it happens
The sun and the moon reappear
The clouds still not in sight
However, it gets darker
Even though it is not stronger than the sun

Suddenly tears of sadness splat down
The clouds were crying
Soon it was dried by the sun
Then whooshed off by the moon

Immediately the sky was completely dark
There was no sun
There was no moon
There were only clouds
But not just clouds
Evil, curious and dark clouds

Now you see
A flash of lightning
A roar of thunder
And the curious-looking faces of clouds.

Denesh Kannalingam (11)
Valentines High School, Ilford

SNOWFALL

Another season yet
Blanketed us with a great white net
Said to be just a show
Oh now it twinkles in the moonlight
Yes, it's snow!

And as I run
Out comes the sun
For all of today
Has suddenly melted away

A season of pure white
Made my heart from dark to light
It helped me share
My feelings and care

Colder than anything before
I could feel the windswept shore
Carry me on my feet
To a lovely cosy sleep

And when I wake up
Who is there?
Not the snow
But lakes with hares

I shed a tear
My only fear
When will I see snow again?

Mahnoor Malik (11)
Valentines High School, Ilford

MY BROKEN HEART

They tell me that I shouldn't
And my heart just felt so wooden
They told me that I couldn't
But I held on to my pendant
I've made it so long and I can't return
If I plead, I should, then I will feel the burn
They broke my heart, split it into pieces
If I tell him the truth all he does is tease

I've told everyone I know
And I've become a foe
I have no one left
And I'm losing control, save me from my death
Leave me in a paradise
I want to be free, nothing's a surprise

All my pages turned, my time is at an end
I have no peace or even a friend
I saw my family die in front of my eyes
I was so scared I heard their war cries
I'm in distress, I'm about to die
These are my final words
Time to say goodbye
I told the truth I received a lie
I stare at the ground and begin to cry.

Arda Kuskaya
Valentines High School, Ilford

THE SEASIDE

In the astonishing sunlit sky
The sky appears as a cake with purple frosting and orange layers
And the sun is the cherry on top
While the seaside is a beautiful place to admire
The tumbling waves crash exuberantly on the salt soaked shore
Not a soul would enter the world of boredom
In the distance the children are giggling with joy
And the crackle of sand as the sandcastles are knocked over by water
The silky smooth blue waves glide across the ocean glamorously
The salty water absorbs into the astounding gold glimmering sand
While the crabs curiously wander sideways
People pick up shells and watch them glint in the flamboyant sky
While there is a war between the wild surfers and the monstrous waves
The sun sets on the horizon
The joyful merry music stops
The umbrellas frantically shut closed
The smoothie bar's shutters drop down making a loud *thud!*
Soon after everyone hears endless moaning of children
The sobbing of babies
The waves become more tranquil
The beaming moon conquers the sunlight
Nothing remains but the forsaken sea, the sand and the moonlight . . .

Zaid Shanawaz (12)
Valentines High School, Ilford

FAMILY IS ALL I NEED

I love my family
I love them more than myself
I can't imagine to see one hurt
I'd do anything to protect them
They're part of me
I'm part of them
I'd be nothing without them.

Ria A Gola (11)
Valentines High School, Ilford

LIFE

You'll only get one shot
No matter what
Inevitably your end will come
And you may feel numb

I am full of sensations
And for every person I have different foundations
I am full of surprises
Some are prizes
Others ensure a problem arises

Whether you lose someone dear
Or it's a moment of fear
If life's a breeze and all is at ease
Or if you knock over a nest of bees
If you manage to stay sane
Or surrender to pain

If you abuse your chance you won't have me any longer
And that won't make you any stronger
When I leave you you're in a grave
So you'd better behave
When I leave you you'll draw your last breath
And then you'll face my opposite, death.

Hussain Seedat (11)
Valentines High School, Ilford

FRIENDS FOR LIFE!

F riends forever in life
R eal friends are the ones that love you
I f we are friends we have to be truthful
E njoy every second we have with one another
N ever-ending friendship
D epend on each other
S tand by each other when we need help.

Harjeevan Panesar (11)
Valentines High School, Ilford

THE SAD TREE

I stand there watching kids play
Running round and round me
I see them and think
How I wish I could run and move
More than just being a tree

I wish I had a mouth to talk
I wish I had legs to walk
But all I am is a standing tree

All kids say, 'Come let's play
Pick leaves from that tree
And play with it!'
All kids walk and run up to me

'Ouch! Ouch!' I say when my leaves get torn off me
And all they leave is an empty branch of the tree
Autumn comes soon and all my precious leaves fall anyway
But what's the point?
I am going to be cut down later in the day.

This is a story of a sad tree
Wishing to have a life
More than just being a sad standing tree.

Tanisa Karim (11)
Valentines High School, Ilford

MY FRIEND

My friend, oh my friend
Your sight is like my light
Oh my friend
I love you above the world
Because you're my best friend
My friend, oh my friend
I love you above the world.

Dev Vora (12)
Valentines High School, Ilford

OCEANS APART

There's a girl over there
I've never seen her before
She always seems sad
Her clothes are torn

People laugh at her hair
Just because it's not fair
Her skin is dark
People say she's odd

I know she's like us
She has feelings and a heart
So I bring myself together
And I go and talk to her

It transpires everyone's wrong
She's actually as kind as can be
Hates being the new girl
That used to be me

She's been called racist names
She comes from afar
She's a refugee from Africa
This is how she met me.

Sophie Midlane (12)
Valentines High School, Ilford

SECRETS

S ilent whispers in your mind
E choing repeatedly
C rawling out of your lips
R eady to burst out aloud
E veryone trying to hear
T hose little words only you know
S pinning in your head, should they know?

Sasha Sood (11)
Valentines High School, Ilford

I'M A CHILD OF A REFUGEE

What world are we all living in?
The terrible, nasty world
We are not at fault
But yet we don't receive our basic human rights
Like everyone in the west

Look around you and where you live
Have you seen at least one country that has not been part of a war?
By 2015, there have been 250 major wars
50 million people killed
Imagine if that was you, dead

You may be lucky now
But what will happen in the future?
There may be a time where you need help
But there will be no one listening
Just like no one is listening to us

We are walking on barefoot to reach a safe destination
It's like we are trapped in this bottle and nobody can rescue us
Yet you people are just watching us suffer
This war, when will it stop, when can I return?
I am the child of a refugee.

Jaha Falak Khan
Valentines High School, Ilford

APPLE PIE

When you see an apple
What is the first thing that comes to mind?
For me it's crispy apple pie

When you take your first tender bite
The apple sauce invades your taste buds
Like an army of warm apple.

Mohammad Sheriff (12)
Valentines High School, Ilford

ALL ABOUT ME

I am a boy who is cool
Who goes to school
But I'm not a fool
I like to laugh
I don't wear a scarf
I eat pie
That doesn't make me fly
I'm also totally not a spy!

Cars are things my parents buy
But when I'm sad I sigh
Now you know all about me
So now can you see
That my enemies will start to flee
They all come to me because they know I'm the man
For breakfast I have toast with jam
Cannot ever get scammed
Or you will be banned
You may fight
But I shall smite
That is the end so goodbye!

Arjun Jandu (12)
Valentines High School, Ilford

SUMMER HOLIDAYS

It's the summer holidays
We can do whatever we want to do
Like playing video games, studying science,
Going to a friend's house
Watching movies

You could go to Valentines Park
And Westfield at Stratford
Don't be too happy
Because you have to do your homework.

Hemang Warudkar (11)
Valentines High School, Ilford

SEASON'S BEAUTY

Whoosh!
While the weakly shining sun appears
The silent sound of falling crystal snowflakes
Does not reach my ears
The cold, unforgiving wind sweeps by
As the skeletal trees, bare of their leaves
Stand guard, tall, yet dry
They dominate the smooth, white blanket
But night has fallen
And the stalking predators are taking control

Chirp!
The soft, sweet song belonging to birds
Fills the air, carrying over the distance
So that all ears heard
Blooming buds grow, swaying in the breeze
As all kinds of bugs, crawling, buzzing, flying
Perch on crisp, lime leaves
Brilliant, beaming, blazing rays
Glare from the horizon
Brightening the entire world so all can see.

Nikita Abedin (11)
Valentines High School, Ilford

HAPPINESS

H olly trees make me pleased
A nd tulips make me proud
P oppies make me delighted and
P ansies peek over the green grass
I ndigo flowers are the best
N ectar from the plants and
E merald green grass shines upon the nature
S tars shining above the field and
S eas reflect on the vibrant colours.

Rabeena Raveendrakumar
Valentines High School, Ilford

POEM ABOUT FANTASY

What is fantasy?
Fantasy is your destiny, it is a mystery
Where can I find fantasy?
Fantasy is in your mind full of your memory

Fantasy can be made
So don't be afraid,
It's like drinking lemonade
So do not be against

Fantasy cannot be snatched
Nor can it be stopped,
If it does, take off your badge
Next time keep it safe, not chopped

Full of mystery
And contains your destiny,
Never can you stop it
Then start to enjoy it,
And never will it stop
So say, 'I believe'
You will forever stay young.

Urbi Haidar (12)
Valentines High School, Ilford

A BEAUTIFUL LIFE

A beautiful life, life is joyful
Life is fun, life brings happiness, life brings love
I'm loved by my mother, I'm loved by my sister
I'm loved by my father, who all give me strength

A beautiful life, I learn new things
Which show me the way of life
It grows and expands as we enjoy friends' time

Enjoy your day as it brings bright colours to your life
A beautiful life, what a wonderful phrase!

Imran Ibrahim (11)
Valentines High School, Ilford

FIREWORKS

Millions and millions of them
All different shapes and sizes
A huge variety of colours
Red and yellow and orange and green and blue

Lighting them up one by one
Letting them go one by one
Seeing them explode
In the dark charcoal black sky
An amazing sight to witness!

People smiling and cheering
Despite the loud hearing
As they are about to touch the sky
Especially on New Year's Day and Diwali
Make it even more great

Never forgetting these excellent times
Listening to the loud noises
As they deafen my ears
Although they are good moments
Happy times are the best!

Neil Patel (11)
Valentines High School, Ilford

WINTER

W onderful, white, crystally snow
 I see shimmery, glass, beautiful icicles
N othing but footprints on the shimmery snow
T ough snow and wind across your face
 E ast, north, south, west filled with snow and busy roads
 R umbling snow tumbling from the cloudy grey sky.

Khadiza Rahman (11)
Valentines High School, Ilford

FLOWER VS BOMB

We never throw a flower
But we can always throw a bomb
Out of every one our world is the one suffering
Individual and whole
We always show the red flag but never the white
If we just show the symbol
The dove symbol
Not even some love would hurt

We were born with love
So let's use it
What's good if we
All just hate it
It comes from within
For once wouldn't you like to be loved

Stop please
Stop living in the dark corner
People are there for a reason
Live in the light, have some fun
But first throw a flower.

Abida Yasminn (11)
Valentines High School, Ilford

POLICEMAN

There was a policeman called Mark
He saw a guy carrying a shark
Mark took him to jail
In his room he was the only male
The next day Mark
Had a trip to the isolated park.

Kamal Shoble
Valentines High School, Ilford

CHOICES POEM

If life leads you the wrong path
You won't be able to turn back
No matter what choice you make
Even if it's a mistake

Life is full of choices
Whether you're on your own
Or picking a friend
Something you can't commend

Listen to your voices
Listen to every sound
They won't let you down
Every day is the beginning of a new chapter
I followed my heart through
All thanks to you
Until this very day
I am me
And you are you
And I am through.

Lina Khemili (12)
Valentines High School, Ilford

FROZEN IN TIME

There I was,
Standing,
Frozen in time.

I was trembling,
But unable to move,
Frozen in time.

Time passed by,
Tick-tock,
Frozen in time.

Unable to move I had just not given up hope.

Yash Dhamija (12)
Valentines High School, Ilford

WHEN YOU ARE OLD

When you are old and grey and full of sleep
And you sit by the burning fire
You see this amazing-looking book
And slowly flick through the pages
And you slowly close your eyes and dream away

You dream about what a great time you had in the past
You dream about when you met the Queen
Then you dream about when you were on stage in front of millions of people
Your heart is beating, time is passing slowly

You are getting nervous as you go to the king to collect your gold medal
Everyone is watching, you're waiting and waiting
And before you know it they call your name
Lights are flashing on people's phones

When you are old you cannot do lots of things
But you wish you could restart your life all over again.

Danis Maninathan
Valentines High School, Ilford

HOMELESS

Walking past the homeless
As our hearts melt with guilt
They ask for money
But we act like we're skint
Tears run down their filthy pale skin
We know we just committed a dirty sin
Just like their hands
Their tummy roaring with hunger
As a cold shiver runs down their spine
Who are they?
They are us!

Amina Mumtaz Qaisar (12)
Valentines High School, Ilford

LIVING IN FEAR

Have you ever been crammed in a dark room
Wondering whether you're going to live or die?
For us, it's our everyday lifestyle
All we can think about is
If we're going to make it to our next birthday
Or if we're going to be grabbed by our legs
Scrunched up into a ball and then eaten
These mysterious creatures
That many people believed to be extinct
Are called Titans, some skinny, some fat
Some with no arms but very interesting faces
They are what we hide from day and night for many months
All we rely on are the survey corps
They fought for us for days and weeks
Until there wasn't one in sight.
But who will fight for humanity when they've all perished? Who will win the world back for us?
We will. Humanity. Together.

Sydney Massey (11)
Valentines High School, Ilford

WINTER DAYS

The days are snowy
It is freezing cold
Can't go out
But someone does
It tempts us

When we do
The snow comes fast
Our minds say, 'Get in fast
Don't even look back, go in fast
Go to the heater as fast as you can.'

Renyl Rathan Selwyn (11)
Valentines High School, Ilford

THERE BUT NOT

If the point of having friends is to not be lonely
Then where are they?
Why do they talk to each other but it's me only?
They ignore me every day
Trying to stand out when they are as great as light
Leaving me dull as darkness
The ignorance is killing me, making me shout and fight!
But alone I am still
I feel like they know what I'm saying but don't hear
As if I'm mute
They don't see me, hear me, notice me even though I'm always near
Do they even try?
We all like the same things, music, movies, subjects and shows
But they don't hear my views
And they invited me into their circle, that's what I know
They were the first friends I had
They are human and I'm entertained by them but
It's like I'm there but not.

Veda Jayne Harrison (12)
Valentines High School, Ilford

LIFE

Take my heart away with my soul
Leave me in a corner, weak, alone
You spit your venom
And take away my pride
And then you will walk away, bye!

Warda Naman (13)
Valentines High School, Ilford

VAMPIRES ARE EVIL!

V ampires are vicious
A nd love everything precious, so be
M indful of the things you keep in your room because on Halloween they will take a
P eek in your house and
I f everything is not hidden, you will want to get
R evenge on the spooky, evil, vicious vampires, even though it was your fault and
E ven when you know that they
S uck your blood if you mess with them

A nd you don't want that! So to get
R evenge, you must be brave, you must be smart and you will
E ventually get the most

E asiest revenge on the
V ampires
I n the whole wide world and everyone will
L ove and respect you!

Nakhal Furqan (11)
Valentines High School, Ilford

SHINY

S ummer is when it is shiny and when the sun is out
H owling in the wind is no more
I always go out in the park to play football
N ever will I not go to the park
Y ou should always go out when it is sunny and shiny.

Yusuf Khankhara (11)
Valentines High School, Ilford

FOOD

Day after day
Night after night
Taken from our families
And then skinned alive
They fry us
They boil us
They toss us around
Insignificant
As they gobble us down
A sizzle
A crackle
A sibling deceased
Then they tear us apart
Right at the seams

The time has come
Dinner time is here
Now it's not very long until I disappear.

Jeni Tanushi (11)
Valentines High School, Ilford

PINK CHERRIES – HAIKU

Look, the cherry tree
Has no cherries. What happened?
The rain has not stopped.

Amelia Hynds (12)
Valentines High School, Ilford

THE WALK

As an affection towards others
She wanders down the catwalk
Her confidence blowing back her hair
As if it's a strong breeze
Up there, with glamour and confidence
People wish they could be like her
Cameras flash at the beautiful sight
The cheers of their loyal fans
Light up their worlds

Living that luxurious life
Expected to love yourself
How they try to be role models
But are never respected
Having the opportunity to travel the world
The blinding light of the camera
Makes her feel good about herself
Because that's her home, her true passion.

Zaiba Adam (12)
Valentines High School, Ilford

SILENCE

I can't live without you
You don't seem to care
Our life together I drew
You've left me struggling for air

I've used up all my wishes
Wishing for you to be by my side
Waiting for your kisses
Or do you want me to die?

You'll never know the endless nights
The pouring of the rain
Always getting myself into fights
To try and wash the pain away

I will never get over you
You think our life together is done
But have you ever had the feeling
That you think about life and say, 'I'm done?'

Jeremy Sanchez-Londono (12)
Valentines High School, Ilford

MY HOLIDAY

Summer holiday is gone,
It was really fun.
I went to lots of places,
And had a great time.

I stayed with my cousins,
And had a sleepover.
We had lots of fun,
And I will never forget that time.

We had lots of parties,
And invited our friends.
It was really exciting,
I will never forget that fun.

As soon as we get sleepy,
We go to our bed.
When we wake up,
We have some fun.

Elise Hassan Islam (12)
Valentines High School, Ilford

BEACH POEM

The beach is a treasure chest
Of pearl and silver shells
Some smaller than my fingernails
Like tiny orange bells

Small, rough, rugged rocks
Glistening in the light
Smooth silky pebbles
In black, grey and white

The beach is a treasure chest
With many kinds of jewels
Like diamonds shining in the sands
Or hiding in rock pools.

Kirit Sehmbi
Valentines High School, Ilford

SWEETS POEM

A bowl of candy, a bowl of treats
A dish of tasty sugary sweets
Chewing nice delicious flavours it's so sweet
What shall I eat?

It tastes like a candy cane waiting to be eaten by someone
It's so yummy to eat a sweet
It's the sweetest dessert there is
It is as sweet as chocolate
It is chewy like gum in a mouth
It's sticky inside
It is easy to make sweets using ingredients

They have all got different tastes and looks
Some are sour, some are sweet
Sweets are nice and sugary and melt in your mouth when you eat them
Sweets are tasty and sweet to eat.

Elisha Nansri Bailey (11)
Valentines High School, Ilford

FAMILY FOREVER

Forever together
Always here for each other
I miss them all the time
They are very kind
I hate my cousin Daisy
Because she is so lazy
My brother likes to rap
While I take a nap
My cousin is so fat
Whenever we play cricket, she always uses my bat
Her name is Maria
But Mary is what we call her
She jumps a lot, to get taller.

Ibraheem Ansari (12)
Valentines High School, Ilford

I WISH FOR A WORLD OF PEACE

I wish for a world of peace
Where there is no difference between rich and poor
Where there is a spot for happiness

But nothing else but kindness
Where everyone knows you can't buy happiness with money
I wish for a world of peace

Joy and fun
For everyone
No sadness or tears
But laughter and no fears

I wish for a world of peace
Kindness
Happiness
And joy – a world of peace

A world of peace!

Tringa Baca
Valentines High School, Ilford

LOVE AUTUMN

All leaves falling on the ground
Kids jumping around

The time goes quick when the wind goes by
But try not to make it fly

Make the most of the red leaves
Because trees want them to breathe

You can just fall in bed
Thinking what people said

Autumn is waiting out there
Just like a bear

Jump around in the leaves
Like you've never seen it before

You will love it for sure
Because it's autumn . . .

Zainah Hussain (11)
Valentines High School, Ilford

LEAVES OF LIFE

The trees are stalling
The leaves are falling
Just like a mill
Nature just won't stay still

The sun is down
Everyone has a frown
They all wear casual gowns
And no one leaves town

The windows are frosty
They look very costly
They sure are pasty
But not so tasty

Weather is nature's gift
It might not give you a lift
But should still be appreciated.

Hassan Mahmood (11)
Valentines High School, Ilford

SECONDARY SCHOOL

V alentines High School is a phenomenal school to be a part of,
A t Valentines I always feel safe and cared for.
L earning at the school is at a high standard and it's taken seriously.
E very subject is fun and so far I have learnt so much it is unbelievable. Although,
N ot every teacher is the nicest, most are and they do their job well.
T o know I am part of a caring and supporting community it gives me hope that...
I will one day be able to give that back to the world.
N aturally I think Valentines will take me a long way.
E verybody might not agree but I think Valentines will change my life,
S econdary school has been a massive change in my life and it is wonderful.

Shaheera Uddin (11)
Valentines High School, Ilford

FOOTBALL POEM

Football is my favourite game
I love to watch contenders play
The free kicks, the skills, the shots
On the awesome match day
How speedily they zoom across the pitch
Such skillful play
Probably the best I've ever seen

People think I'm insane
The way I admire the game
But the only thing I'd want to do
Is to watch the game more than anything I can think of
Of course I have a team
Manchester United
The great team that dominates the league
The Devils.

Mohammed Zaid Kidia (11)
Valentines High School, Ilford

FRIENDS FOREVER

F riends are forever, always stay together
R eunited if separated
I f you're ever lonely
E very time they will be there
N ever, ever let you down
D on't ever make you frown
S pecial friends forever

F orever we are friends
O h it will never end
R emember us forever and
E ver
V ersatile and different but that never
E ver parts us
R espect each other we are friends forever.

Umar Salam (11)
Valentines High School, Ilford

WINTER ...

After about three quarters of the year
Finally winter has made its way here
As I slowly move my head and look up high
I see soft white snowflakes falling from the sky

Snowy mountains and frozen lakes
All covered in white sparkling snowflakes
The windy winter breeze hits my face
Whilst ice skating happily, always with grace

Making snow angels and skiing downhill
Landing in snow and getting a chill
Building snowmen and having a snowball fight
Winter is here – what a wonderful sight

The cold bit my mind but my heart said it's fine
It's only just a winter sign.

Maheen Khalid (12)
Valentines High School, Ilford

NATURE'S CREATION

The birds are whining
The sun is shining
The river is crying
The ground is cracking
And so am I!

The wind is blowing
The trees are grabbing
The mountains are stamping
And so am I!

The owl is howling
The branches are crunching
The moon is rising
The ocean is sleeping
And so am I!

Luqmaan Khan (11)
Valentines High School, Ilford

A ROOM WITH NO DOORS

I feel like I'm stuck in a room with no doors
No lights or windows, just walls and floors
My dad doesn't see us much anymore
Probably doesn't even know that we're poor

'My mum's amazing,' I've always said
She makes me food and puts a roof over my head
But Mum's sweet smile only hid depression
A lifetime of guilt and counselling sessions

My mother is unemployed
My brother is heartbroken and we're all lost in a void
In 2013 I was diagnosed with anxiety
I have to take pills and I thank Raz for getting by with me

I think it sucks that the council gives us money
You see, it's not enough, and it makes my mother sad
And if I catch myself crying I always find it funny
I'd just sit there alone; mourning the life that I once had

But one thing I don't want is sympathy
Because I know somewhere in the world, somebody's got it worse than me
Me and my family struggle – money, divorce and anxiety
A room with no doors
And you see, it's not all bad
Every morning my mum wakes me up
She'll give a bit of hot chocolate in a cute Disney cup
And then she'd smile gently and give me a hug
A hug full of so much love I nearly drop my Disney mug

And she'd put on a film if we could afford treats
We'd put on The Hangover Part 1 and I'd see her laugh as she eats
And when she makes me lunch, she cuts off the crusts
'Just how I like it,' I'd say as we'd discuss
My GCSE and my new English score

I don't need money or my old life anymore
Being with my mother is my room's hidden door.

Amy Harland (14)
Westfield Academy, Watford

Est. 1991

YOUNG WRITERS INFORMATION

We hope you have enjoyed reading this book – and that you will continue to in the coming years.

If you're a young writer who enjoys reading and creative writing, or the parent of an enthusiastic poet or story writer, do visit our website www.youngwriters.co.uk. Here you will find free competitions, workshops and games, as well as recommended reads, a poetry glossary and our blog.

If you would like to order further copies of this book, or any of our other titles give us a call or visit **www.youngwriters.co.uk**.

Young Writers
Remus House
Coltsfoot Drive
Peterborough
PE2 9BF

(01733) 890066
info@youngwriters.co.uk